Learning Resources Centre
JFS School
The Mall
Kenton
Harrow
HA3 9TE

FOR REFERENCE ONLY

A Classification System for Libraries of Judaica

A Classification System for Libraries of Judaica

David H. Elazar
Daniel J. Elazar

WITH THE ASSISTANCE OF
Rachel K. Glasser
Rita B. Frischer

A Jason Aronson Book

ROWMAN & LITTLEFIELD PUBLISHERS, INC.
Lanham • Boulder • New York • Toronto • Plymouth, UK

A JASON ARONSON BOOK

ROWMAN & LITTLEFIELD PUBLISHERS, INC.

Published in the United States of America
by Rowman & Littlefield Publishers, Inc.
A wholly owned subsidiary of The Rowman & Littlefield Publishing Group, Inc.
4501 Forbes Boulevard, Suite 200, Lanham, Maryland 20706
www.rowmanlittlefield.com

Estover Road
Plymouth PL6 7PY
United Kingdom

ISBN: 0-7657-5983-7

*Dedicated to the United Hebrew Schools
of Metropolitan Detroit,
where this classification system originated.
And, to our father,
the late Albert Elazar,
and his colleagues, who, together,
made these schools the strongest Jewish
supplementary educational system in the United States,
and a beacon and symbol of the best the
Jewish community has to offer
in its pursuit of national and cultural ideals.*

Contents

Preface		ix
Introduction		1
Classifying a Book		17
Summary		25
001–099	Bible and Biblical Studies	31
100–199	Classical Judaica: Halakhah and Midrash	47
200–299	Jewish Observance and Practice	69
300–399	Jewish Education	85
400–499	Hebrew, Jewish Languages, and Sciences	95
500–599	Jewish Literature	103
600–699	The Jewish Community: Society and the Arts	111
700–799	Jewish History, Geography, Biography	129
800–899	Israel and Zionism	145
900–999	General Works	171
Index		181

Preface

Invented and first applied in 1952, the first published edition of this classification system appeared in 1962. Since then, its use has spread widely throughout the United States, Israel, and other parts of the Jewish world. Libraries of all kinds, in synagogues and community centers, in Hebrew schools, on college campuses and in research institutions, have adopted the scheme and worked with it. As a result, a body of experience in applying the system to all these diverse institutions developed, clearly demonstrating the need for minimal changes in the system from time to time while reaffirming the utility of its basic organizing principles. Meanwhile, the intervening years have been full of events deeply significant in contemporary Jewish history, all of which need to be reflected in an up-to-date classification scheme.

Now, as the system reaches the mid-way point of its fifth decade, we are pleased to issue this Third Revised Edition, which incorporates the lessons of experience in the field and seeks to satisfy the new bibliographic needs generated in the years since its invention and initial application. No major changes have been made as were done with the 500s in the last edition. Rather, these revisions are designed specifically to expand and clarify the system and make it more current and easier to use.

In this edition, subjects have been added and certain divisions, especially the 700s and 800s, were updated as required. The index has been expanded to make it more useful and accurate. Our authority is now the multivolume *Encyclopaedia Judaica* (Keter 1972). However, there are certain exceptions; for example, for names of organizations and persons, we use the accepted spelling as used by the organization or person.

History and Scope

The classification system presented in the following pages was developed for use in the Library of the United Hebrew Schools of Detroit, Michigan. First drafted in 1952, it has been in use there through several revisions and numerous modifications. The United Hebrew Schools Library served elementary, high school, and college students; teachers on all levels; and the Jewish community at large. It was an ideal setting for testing and refining a system that organizes the published literature of Jewish civilization in all its aspects.

The original published 1962 edition of the classification system contained many modifications to the 1952 draft based on the experiences of the librarians and patrons of the United Hebrew Schools Library. Their aid was invaluable and their share in the development of this system should be recognized. Particular acknowledgment must be made to the late Albert Elazar and Isadore Goldstein, then respectively superintendent and administrative secretary of the United Hebrew Schools. Their encouragement and active support of the Library and of the authors during their tenure as librarians there were decisive in making the publication of this system possible.

Prior to publication of the first edition in 1962, a mimeographed draft version of this system was circulated for comment and criticism through the assistance of the National Foundation for Jewish Culture. Thanks are due the Foundation and particularly the late Judah J. Shapiro, then its executive secretary, for making that developmental step possible. We are also grateful to the Wayne State University Graduate Division for providing a grant-in-aid that was used toward preparing the manuscript for publication and to Dr. G. Flint Purdy, Director of Libraries, for help in securing publication of the first edition by Wayne State University Libraries. We owe much to that institution for making our system available and for handling its distribution during its first published decade.

The second edition, published in 1978 with an addenda added in 1988, was based largely on the comments of the members of the Association of Jewish Libraries of Southern California. These librarians systematically responded to our request for feedback, thereby enabling us to produce what we believe were more effective revisions than would otherwise have been the case. We are particularly gratified that the Los Angeles area, with its strong chapter of the International Association of Jewish Libraries, has come to rely heavily on our classification system. For these earlier editions, we are grateful to the late Dorothy Schroeder, to Adaire Klein, and to Barbara Leff, who encouraged us to undertake the revisions and served as links between us and their constituency. Responsibility for the publication and distribution of the system was passed to the Jerusalem Center for Public Affairs; actual publication was undertaken jointly by the Center and the University Press of America.

In the preparation of this Third Revised Edition of the Elazar Classification System, we have been assisted by two of its most experienced advocates in the field, Rita B. Frischer and Rachel K. Glasser of Sinai Temple Blumenthal Library and the Central

Cataloging Service for Libraries of Judaica (CCS) in Los Angeles. They have recommended changes, contributed suggestions and expanded notes to make the scheme easier to use, reworked the index, and reviewed the whole manuscript in light of their experience and that of their colleagues. We have benefitted significantly from their efforts. We also acknowledge the important role CCS has played in Judaica librarianship since 1986, supporting and encouraging a high standard of Judaic cataloging while advocating the Elazar Classification System as a valuable tool in achieving that goal.

David H. Elazar and Daniel J. Elazar
Rishon le-Zion and Jerusalem

Introduction

The rapid and gratifying expansion of Jewish libraries and library services at all levels in the postwar period made the long existing need for a simple yet comprehensive means to organize the Jewish book collection even more apparent. Until the invention of this system, Jewish libraries either used locally devised schemes or had to adapt bits and pieces of general classification systems for their purposes. Because most of the great libraries of Judaica are housed within general libraries, such as the Library of Congress or the New York Public Library, or form the central core of general collections, as in the case of the Jewish National and Hebrew University Library, adaptations of this kind have been reasonably well suited to their needs. Consequently, the contributions of those libraries to the development of Jewish classification schemes have been confined to refining the subsections of general classification systems so that Judaica materials can be better subdivided within the overall framework of human knowledge.

The development of libraries exclusively devoted to the collection and dissemination of Judaica has rendered such stop-gap measures inadequate. The sheer range of materials that such libraries must handle requires more easily accessible classification space than the other systems can provide. Indeed, the development of these specialized libraries offers concrete evidence to support what should have been self-evident: that Jewish civilization covers such a wide range of concerns that the written works it produces can easily support a full classification system devoted only to Judaica.

Aside from this difficulty, there is a problem of potentially greater import. The classification systems that are no more than variations of Dewey or the Library of Congress must perforce fit Judaica materials in the procrustean (or Sodomian) bed of Western civilization. This has two unfavorable consequences, one technical and one substantive. Technically, these systems are either confined to the classical Judaica of biblical studies and Talmudics or simply consist of call numbers for the classification of Judaica materials in locations throughout the general system wherever they fit into the general scheme (e.g., materials on the State of Israel use the appropriate numbers under geography, whereas materials on Jewish literature are classified using numbers located throughout the world literature section). The pattern that emerges from this approach either serves to scatter Judaica materials throughout a general collection or, in an exclusively Jewish library, creates a highly unsystematic and even confusing arrangement of books classified on the basis of numbers abstracted without reference to any meaningfully Jewish integrating principles.

The latter question relates directly to the substantive problem. Using all or parts of a general system prevents the organization of Jewish library materials around Jewish principles. Although the first task of a classification system is the obvious technical one of providing an efficient means for arrangement and retrieval of library materials, it is our belief that a good system has an educational function to serve as well. A good Judaica classification system must give the librarian, and the reader, some direction for approaching Jewish materials, as well as a convenient way to find those materials. Ideally, then, a classification system should not be just an arbitrary arrangement but a calculated means for organizing knowledge in its field. And any attempt to organize knowledge must be rooted in the fundamental principles of the field it seeks to organize. The classification system presented in the following pages embodies every effort to encompass the range of Jewish knowledge found in the kinds of published materials now located in libraries, ranging from books to the latest materials in electronic format. Although based on the familiar decimal organization, and to that extent tied to the canons of Western logic, the categories, their sequence, and the terminology employed to label them are drawn from Jewish tradition insofar as possible. This had meant the construction of a system "from the ground up," as it were, beginning with certain conceptions about the proper way to organize Jewish knowledge and the appropriate categories for its division. The organizational principles of the system devised, as they have been crystallized after 15 years of testing in the United Hebrew Schools Library in Detroit, should be reasonably self-evident. Accordingly, the explanation included here has been kept to a minimum.

The system is structured around the following ten classes:

001–099	Bible and Biblical Studies
100–199	Classical Judaica: Halakhah and Midrash
200–299	Jewish Observance and Practice
300–399	Jewish Education
400–499	Hebrew, Jewish Languages and Sciences
500–599	Jewish Literature
600–699	The Jewish Community: Society and the Arts
700–799	Jewish History, Geography, Biography
800–899	Israel and Zionism
900–999	General Works

Some sense of the internal logic of this arrangement should be immediately apparent, although the linear organization of the materials functions to obscure it. Its essence is the idea that, in Jewish life as a whole and in every field within it, knowledge is organized around a core subject to which related materials accrete with the passage of time, sometimes being added to the basic subject matter in what seem to be concentric circles, and sometimes seemingly penetrating previously created circles to return to immediate contact with the original core.

1. The Bible is the heart of hearts—the core of cores—of the entire body of Jewish knowledge, which, like all Jewish life, is ultimately rooted in the Book of Books. Whether one's immediate concern is with Jewish law, Jewish history, the Hebrew language, or modern Israel—to name only a few of the myriad concerns of Jewish civilization—one is ultimately thrust back to that source. Consequently the Bible and those elements of knowledge that directly elucidate its meaning must be at the core of any Jewish system of classification. In a linear system, this means it must come first.

Within the framework of Bible and biblical studies, movement is multifaceted: from traditional commentaries to modern critical research; from the Torah to the *Nevi'im* (Prophets) to the *Ketuvim* (Writings); from canonical materials to the non-canonical works of the Apocrypha and Pseudepigrapha, which elucidate biblical themes; and from materials directly concerned with the Bible and its immediate environment to those that deal with the Bible in its larger setting. Within the confines of linear structure, the following divisions were designed to handle those progressions:

    001   Complete Bible (with traditional translations, commentaries, etc.)
    005   Bible—Research and Criticism
    015   Torah (Pentateuch, Five Books of Moses)

Introduction

025	*Nevi'im* (Prophets)
050	*Ketuvim* (Writings)
070	Apocrypha
080	Pseudepigrapha
090	Ancient Near East

The movements, however, are not only multifaceted but intertwined. Consequently within each division, provision is made for the classification of materials according to the various facets as relevant.

2. Both structurally and historically, the Talmud and its parts, plus those elements of Halakhah, Kabbalah, and Jewish thought that are products or offshoots of the Talmudic system, represent what has come to be called normative Judaism. By successfully claiming the right of normative biblical interpretation, the Talmudists erected a system that has come to be recognized as the classical system of Jewish life and thought. Consequently, it forms the primary circle around the biblical core with the Talmud at its center and occupies the second position in the classification system.

Within the category of Classical Judaica, movement from the Talmudic core is in several concurrent directions, all of which are united by the sense and spirit of *midrash* or the searching out and explication of meaning from the sacred texts. These directions include the two branches of Talmudic thought, halakhah (Jewish law) and aggadah (nonlegal explicatory materials), and the systems of post-Talmudic speculative thought, Kabbalah ("theosophy") and systematic Jewish speculative thought (what is commonly referred to as "Jewish philosophy"). This movement is expressed through the following divisions:

100	Jewish Law, Lore, and Thought
101	Talmud with Traditional Commentaries

110	Mishnah
115	Jerusalem Talmud
120	History and Development of the Gemara
125	Post-Talmudic Halakhah
135	Jewish Thought—General Works
140	Aggadah–Classical Midrash
150	Kabbalah
170	Medieval Jewish Thought
175	Modern Jewish Thought
185	Jewish Folklore

3. Those *mitzvot*, observances, and practices that together compose the Jewish way of life have emerged from normative Judaism; thus the next major class is properly one that embodies the immediately practical expression of the classical Jewish ideas covered in the previous one. Here, too, the linear projection is only partially accurate. Biblical ideas infuse the Jewish way of life directly as well as through the Talmudic system, and Jews have periodically turned directly to the Bible for direction, inspiration, and validation of those elements of Jewish observance and practice in their life cycles. Although that connection is obscured by the linear system, recognition of its existence helps account for the precise position of this category as the third major class.

Movement within the third class should be only minimally linear, because each division actually occupies a segment of the circle that comprises the central core of the Jewish way of life. Consequently, the internal structure of this class focuses on the Jewish calendar, which is at the core of Jewish observance. The final two categories in the class reflect the larger world of which Jews and Judaism are necessarily a part. As a civilization often located among other civilizations and increasingly at home within them, Judaism or various Jewries are absorbing holidays of larger scope (e.g., Thanksgiving in the United

Introduction

States), while our understanding of Jewish religious life is being enhanced through the study of comparative religion.

200	Jewish Religion—General Works
210	Jewish Religious Movements
220	Guides to Jewish Living
230	Jewish Liturgy
235	The Jewish Calendar
270	Special Events and Occasions
290	Comparative Religion

4. From Biblical times, Jews have acknowledged that the perpetuation of their tradition is possible only through an all-encompassing system of Jewish education—an education traditionally rooted in biblical, Talmudic, and classical Judaic studies and geared toward enabling Jews to live a proper Jewish life in the traditional pattern. Placement of materials on Jewish education in the fourth position, then, is entirely with the internal logic of the classification scheme.

The divisions within the class covering Jewish Education follow more familiar canons of organization once the precedence of the Jewish materials is established. Indeed, of all the sections of the classification system, this one is more likely to include a mixture of general as well as Jewish materials by its very nature and given the emphasis of contemporary Jewish libraries. Its divisions are as follows:

300	Jewish Education
307	History of Jewish Education
310	Jewish Education in the United States
315	School Administration
325	Teaching
330	Curriculum
340	Early Childhood Education

345	Elementary and Intermediate Education
355	Secondary Education
365	Higher Education
375	Adult Education
385	Special Education
390	Psychology

5. The character of Jewish education, by the same token, is informed through and by the languages that Jews have used, the Hebrew language being the most important by far. As contemporary students of culture well know, language is the means through which people perceive and organize reality, and particular languages represent different ways of "programming" approaches to ordering reality. Jewish tradition has recognized the importance of language in this regard for at least two millennia. In Jewish thought, language has been considered the mother science and the mother of sciences. Although the concern for sciences in a classification system for Judaica must, of necessity, be minimal and even peripheral, focusing primarily on certain specialized Jewish scientific interests and contributions, such material as is relevant is, from a Jewish point of view, properly placed in the same class with languages.

The internal divisions in this section follow the historical order of precedence for the four most important Jewish languages, with Hebrew first and foremost. They are followed by a division covering less important languages, which are also ordered more or less chronologically considering that many of these languages overlap in time. Finally, the section includes space for comparative linguistics, particularly Semitic and ancient Near Eastern languages, and the sciences as indicated in the preceding paragraph.

400	Hebrew Language
415	Aramaic

Introduction

425	Ladino (Judezimo)
435	Yiddish
445	Other Jewish Languages
455	Semitic and Ancient Near Eastern Languages
470	Comparative Linguistics
480	Sciences

6. From language flows literature, the primary means of organizing those creative potentialities of specifically aesthetic interest contained within every language. Jewish literature as a specialized activity appears rather late in the span of Jewish history. It is subdivided here by approach first and, for each approach, by period, locale, and language.

500	Jewish Literature—History and Development
530	Jewish Literature—Criticism and Analysis
540	Jewish Literature—Study and Teaching
550	Jewish Literature—Anthologies and Selections
560	Jewish Literature—Individual Works
590	General Literature Related to Jews and Judaism

7. The line of development from Bible, the central core of the entire system, through Education and Language more or less terminates with Literature. Hence the next major class, the Jewish Community, represents a return to that core. In this class, the system focuses on the Jewish community in the largest sense, on its social structure and organization, its institutions and habits, and its modes of aesthetic expression other than literature. Its divisions are primarily topical and, in a sense, sequential. Internally, they are further subdivided according to the different locations of specific Jewish communities in time and space, down to classifications by city. The primary divisions are as follows:

600	Jewish Social Institutions and Behavior
610	Personal and Social Customs
620	Jewish Community Structure and Governance
635	Communal Institutions and Organizations
645	Jewish Economic Institutions and Behavior
650	Social Conditions and Problems
660	The Jews in the World Order
670	Jewish Graphic and Plastic Arts
685	Jewish Music
690	Public Entertainment, Mass Media
699	Cooking and Culinary Arts

8. The community, *Klal Yisrael*, has a direct relationship to the great sources of Jewish civilization, and also has an existence of its own beyond that of any of those sources other than the Bible itself. Yet the life of the community is not only expressed through those sources, but through history, the next major class, as well. History, considered here in its largest sense, includes the spatial considerations of geography as well as the usual temporal ones, and the individualized history found in biography.

The divisions of this section follow a system of periodization of Jewish history developed by one of the authors in another connection. A full explanation of that system may be found in the Introduction to Daniel J. Elazar and Stuart A. Cohen, *The Jewish Polity* (Bloomington, IN: Indiana University Press, 1987). For purposes of clarification here, it is sufficient to note that the system is based on the most "Jewishly" significant points of historical change. This is, like the classification system as a whole, based on Jewish, in this case, Jewishly significant events rather than those forced on the Jewish people from the outside. The major divisions in the 700s are those based on the major points of change in the constitution of the Jewish way of life: the rise of the patriarchs; the exodus from Egypt and the constitution of the tribal confederacy; the

Introduction

reorganization of Israel that accompanied the rise of the monarchy; the restoration of the theocratic commonwealth under Ezra and Nehemiah; the assumption of authority by the Pharisees and the introduction of Talmudic Judaism; the codification of the Mishnah and its effective employment at the center of Jewish law; the final shaping of normative Judaism with the completion of the Talmud; the reorganization of Jewish life under the first Codes; the sharpening of normative Judaism by casting its codes in the light of changing ideas of the Middle Ages; the completion and widespread adoption of the *Shulhan Arukh*; and the shattering of the dominance of normative Judaism with the triumph of modernism among the majority of Jews in our own time. The major subdivisions do no more than portray the skeleton of this system, but the titles and dates assigned to specific numbers within them should add further clarification to the few explanatory remarks included here. It should be noted that an abridged version of this system of historical periodization is used within the subdivisions of the 600s.

The divisions also reflect the sociogeographic divisions of the Jewish people encountered earlier. Within them the subject matter is further broken down by country and, in some cases, by state or province as well. Where necessary or desirable, it is possible to classify materials by city or similar local subdivision.

700	Jewish History
710	The Emergence of the Jewish People (20th–5th Centuries BCE)
720	The Emergence of Talmudic Judaism (5th Century BCE–8th Century CE)
730	The Era of Normative Judaism (9th–19th Centuries)
735	The Contemporary Era (20th Century-)

740	The Jews of the Middle East
750	Sephardic and Mediterranean Jewry
760	Ashkenazic and Eastern European Jewry
765	Western European Jewry
770	United States Jewry
785	South American Jewry
790	African Jewry
795	Geography
798	Collective Biography

9. In all of Jewish history, the various elements of Jewish civilization come together as an organic whole only in the land of Israel, which, as a unifying force in Jewish life, properly stands as the polar companion of the Bible. The contemporary character of the land of Israel is the product of the Zionist revolution and its creation, the State of Israel. Hence the focus is on those two aspects of Jewish life in all their details: those of specific and direct concern for the mainstream of Jewish civilization and those that appear, at first glance, to be more general in nature.

The divisions of this section begin with Zionism as a movement, as a system of thought, and as a set of institutions; they then turn to Israel—the class's central core—and, after establishing its temporal and spatial character, examine the State of Israel topically. As in the other classes, this one concludes with the broadest possible perspective: Israel's relationships with world Jewry and the rest of the Middle East.

800	Zionism
805	National Institutions, Zionist Organizational Structure
810	Zionist Parties and Popular Organizations
820	Israel (*Eretz Yisrael*)
830	Israel—Geography
840	Israel—Government and Politics

Introduction 13

855 Israel—Economics and Development
865 Israel—Demography, Population
875 Israel—Culture
880 Israel—Arts
885 Israel and World Jewry
890 Israel and the Middle East

10. The final major class is a synthetic one that incorporates material that crosses the boundaries of the other classes, or which relates to the various modes of organization of the entire range of Jewish knowledge. Following the overall principles of the system, it represents the circle at its broadest expansion away from the narrow biblical core. Here we include the general scholarly tools such as encyclopedias, yearbooks, newspapers and multi-interest periodicals, and bibliographies. Here, too, are located technical materials related to Jewish libraries, archives, and museums and the Jewish book itself. Finally, space is provided in this class for other kinds of library acquisitions, particularly audiovisual materials in various formats (audio and video tapes, CD-ROMs, video disks, etc.) and computer software and programs. Its subdivisions are self-explanatory:

900 Jewish Encyclopedias
910 General Collections of Essays
915 Jewish Yearbooks, Almanacs, Directories
920 Jewish Journalism
940 The Jewish Book
950 Jewish Bibliography
960 Audiovisual Materials
970 Library Science
980 The Jewish Library
995 The Jewish Museum

The scheme of interrelationships, implicit in the foregoing structure, can best be illustrated in the following diagram showing the ten major divisions in nonlinear order and the primary and secondary connections between them.

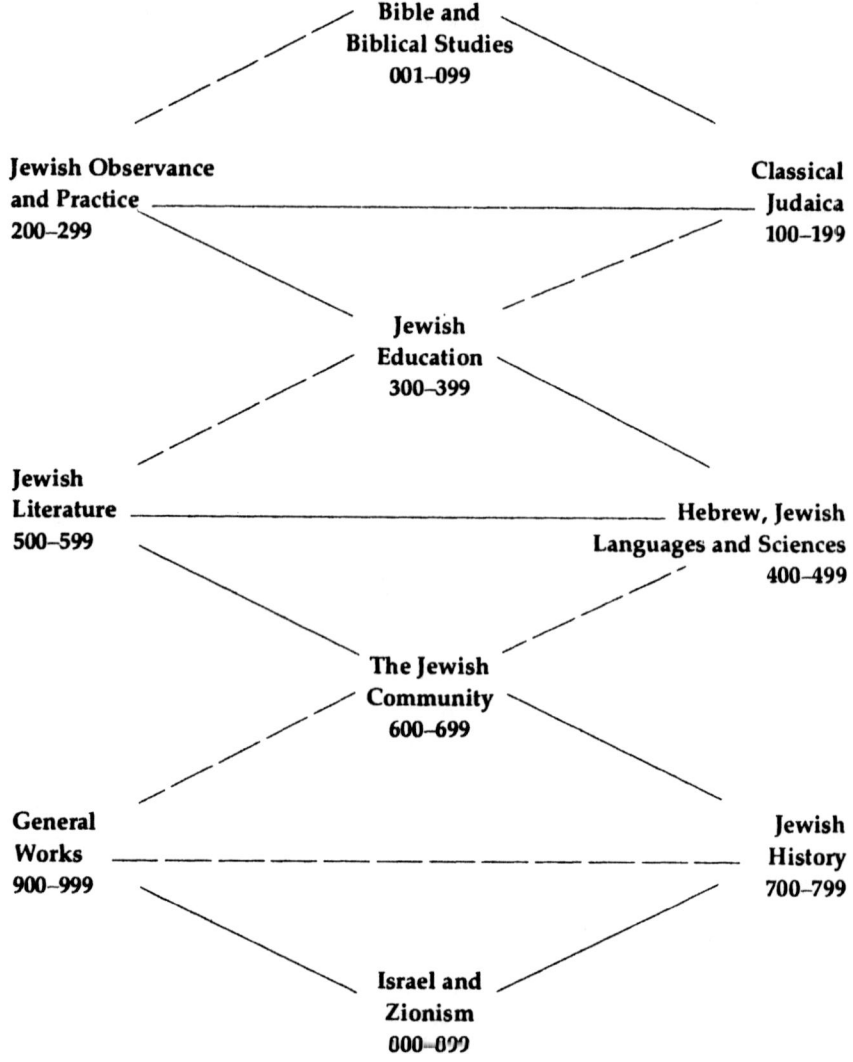

The ten major classes and the ninety-nine divisions within them are designed to elucidate the overall structure of the classification system. However, they may also be used as a complete classification scheme in miniature. In libraries where the Jewish book collection is too limited or the people in charge find detailed classification too difficult, the divisions can be abstracted for separate use with the addition of any of the other numbers an optional matter.

Classifying a Book

Classification Procedure

Proper classification of library materials, whether print or nonprint, is possible only after thorough familiarization with the classification system being used. This includes an understanding of the organization of the system with its major classes and divisions (see Introduction) and the ability to use both the classification tables and the index as a guide.

To determine the main subject of a book, examine the volume very carefully in the following manner:

1. Look at the book title.
2. Check the verso of the title page for Cataloging-In-Publication (CIP) data. This should be used only as a general guide.
3. Examine the table of contents, index, glossary, and bibliographies.
4. Read the foreword, preface, and introduction.
5. Read any available book reviews.

Although this is not a substitute for reading the book, these steps should provide enough information for the classification of most items. Once the subject has been determined, refer to the classification tables for the class number, using the index as a guide. Be sure to follow any instructions or notes concerning the proper use of the number. Because these guidelines are found only within the system itself, the index should never be used for direct assignment of classification numbers.

For "problem" books, one may check to see how other libraries have classified them. Among such sources of classification information are the Library of Congress catalogs (Library of Congress Cataloging Distribution Service, Washington DC 20541), various online (Internet) catalogs, and the Central Cataloging Service for Libraries of Judaica (Sinai Temple Library, 10400 Wilshire Blvd., Los Angeles, CA 90024).

Call Numbers

Every cataloged item in a library (print or nonprint) has its own distinct set of identifying symbols (numbers and letters) according to its place in the classification system.

For example:

> 021.23   Goldman, Solomon   *The Ten Commandments*
> Gol

or

> 021.23   Goldman, Solomon   *The Ten Commandments*
> G 619

021.23 is the classification for modern critical commentaries on The Book of Exodus. Gol or G 619 stand for the author's last name and are known as an author mark or a book number. This combination of the classification number and author mark is the "call number."

Many libraries use only the first three letters of the author's last name as the author mark (Gol). Others prefer to use a combination of letters and numbers as set forth by the standard two-figure or three-figure systems known as the Cutter-Sanborn Author Tables (available on the Internet, or in print and CD-ROM from Libraries Unlimited, Dept. 9555, P.O. Box 6633, Englewood, CO 80155-6633) or the Library of Congress Cutter Tables (available on the Internet). Using these tables lessens the possibility of two books having the same call number. For example, with the LC system Kohen would be represented as K644 and Kohn as K646.

Call numbers using the LC Cutter (2 digits):

181.1 K37	Kaplan, Mordecai	*The Meaning of God in Modern Jewish Religion*
181.1 K64	Kohn, Eugene	*Religion and Humanity*
180.1 B83b	Buber, Martin	*Between Man and Man*
180.1 B83d	Buber, Martin	*Daniel: Dialogues on Realization*

The small "b" and "d" after the author marks in the last two examples stand for the titles of the respective works.

A similar system, using Hebrew characters, exists for placing Hebrew and Yiddish books in order. A guide to this system may be found in Herbert C. Zafran, "Arranging Your Books" (in *Studies in Bibliography and Booklore*, 4(1):3–20, June 1959. Reprints available from Hebrew Union College-JIR Library, 3101 Clifton Ave., Cincinnati, OH 45220). Although this system was invented for cuttering titles in Hebrew, it has also proven successful in the cuttering of authors.

Building Numbers

The note "Divide like 740–796" is found very often in the classification tables. Its purpose is to enable the cataloger to specify a geographic area or local community. Therefore, to classify a book that is concerned with anti-semitism in the United States, two classification numbers would be combined in the following manner:

    662   Anti-semitism
              Divide like 740–796

plus
    770   History of the Jews in the United States

equals
    662.7   Anti-semitism in the United States

The first 7 of 770, which represents the History category, is dropped and the 70, which represents a locality, is added to 662 as a decimal. Since the zero is not needed, it is omitted. Following this pattern, anti-semitism in Russia (764) would be designated 662.64 and anti-semitism in Detroit (775.4) would be 662.754.

Variations in Classification and Special Locations

1. Biography

Although 799 is the designated placement for biographies within the scheme, one might choose to use the letter "B" (or, where Hebrew books are shelved separately, the Hebrew letter "Bet") for individual biographies. Whether using "B" or 799, the next line of the call number is then derived from the name of the subject of the biography rather than that of the author. For example:

B	Lewisohn, Ludwig	799
H5821	*Theodor Herzl*	HER
		Lew

or

B	Cohen, Israel	799
H582c	*Theodor Herzl*	HER
		Coh

When using Cutter, the small letters "l" and "c" stand for the initials of the authors' last names.

2. Fiction

Many libraries prefer to shelve fiction alphabetically by author. Rather than assigning a classification number, use the letter "F" or "FIC" along with the appropriate author mark.

3. Reference

The letter(s) "R" or "REF" are used as a prefix before the classification number to identify material whose removal from the library is restricted.

R		REF
403.2	Alcalay, Rueben	403.2
A42	*Complete Hebrew-English Dictionary*	Alc
1965	1965 edition	

This identification on the spine of the book can also indicate that the book is to be shelved in a specially assigned area when reference and circulating materials are shelved separately.

4. *Juveniles*

These books may be shelved in the children's division of the library and appropriate prefixes should be assigned to reflect various age levels (e.g., j = Juvenile; x = Intermediate; YA = Young Adult).

5. *Hebrew books*

For those libraries where the Hebrew books are not shelved separately from the English ones, the Hebrew character in the author mark can be transliterated into Latin characters and the books interfiled. Even when shelved separately, an "H" prefix aids in shelving, retrieval, and in computer entry and access for those libraries using software limited to Romanization.

6. *Yiddish books*

When assigning author marks for Yiddish books, the system for Hebrew characters should be used. To distinguish the Yiddish from the Hebrew for shelving and computer purposes, prefix the classification number with the letter "Y."

General Materials

Classification of materials with no specifically Jewish content is not provided for in this classification system. When it is the policy of a library to include such material in its collection, a general classification scheme such as the Dewey Decimal Classification (available from OCLC Forest Press, 6565 Frantz Road, Dublin OH 43017-3395) or the Library of Congress system (available from Library of Congress Cataloging Distribution Service, Washington DC 20541) should be used as an adjunct to this scheme. Obviously, this approach may require

Classifying a Book

some differentiation. Jewish day schools frequently use Elazar and Dewey in tandem, assigning a prefix as a marker (e.g., "D" for Dewey before the general class number) and shelving such marked material together in a specially designated section of the library.

Other Special Categories

Although the system provides for various formats within the 960s and for pedagogical aids within the 300s, many libraries with large special usage collections may prefer to assign numbers that reflect the overall scheme. This approach requires specific prefix designations. Among these may be letters denoting a Teachers' Center (T) or Parenting collection (P), as well as prefixes for various audiovisual materials (VCR for videocassette recordings, SL for slides, etc.). Following this model, various materials might be classified as follows:

238	High Holidays
T 238	Teachers' materials on teaching the High Holidays
VCR 238	Videocassettes on High Holidays
652	Adoption
P 652	Material for parents to use specifically when telling children about adoption

Hebrew Transliteration

This classification system bases its Hebrew transliteration on that given in the multivolume *Encyclopaedia Judaica* (Keter

Publishing House, 1972) using the transliteration rules found on page 90 of Volume 1 (Index). However, there are certain exceptions. For names of organizations and persons, use the accepted spelling as used by the respective organization/person. For the Hebrew letter "zadik," use "tz."

Summary

001–099 Bible and Biblical Studies

001	Complete Bible (with traditional translations, commentaries, etc.)
005	Bible—Research and Criticism
015	Torah (Pentateuch, Five Books of Moses)
025	*Nevi'im* (Prophets)
050	*Ketuvim* (Writings)
070	Apocrypha
080	Pseudepigrapha
090	Ancient Near East

100–199 Classical Judaica: Halakhah and Midrash

100	Jewish Law, Lore, and Thought
101	Talmud with Traditional Commentaries
110	Mishnah
115	Jerusalem Talmud
120	History and Development of the Gemarah
125	Post-Talmudic Halakhah
135	Jewish Thought—General Works

140	Aggadah—Classical Midrash
150	Kabbalah
170	Medieval Jewish Thought
175	Modern Jewish Thought
185	Jewish Folklore

200–299 Jewish Observance and Practice

200	Jewish Religion—General Works
210	Jewish Religious Movements
220	Guides to Jewish Living—General Works
230	Jewish Liturgy
235	The Jewish Calendar
270	Special Events and Occasions
290	Comparative Religion

300–399 Jewish Education

300	Jewish Education
307	History of Jewish Education
310	Jewish Education in the United States
315	School Administration
325	Teaching
330	Curriculum
340	Early Childhood Education
345	Elementary and Intermediate Education
355	Secondary Education
365	Higher Education
375	Adult Education

Summary

385 Special Education
390 Psychology

400–499 Hebrew, Jewish Languages, and Sciences

400 Hebrew Language
415 Aramaic
425 Ladino (Judezimo)
435 Yiddish
445 Other Jewish Languages
455 Semitic and Ancient Near Eastern Languages
470 Comparative Linguistics
480 Sciences

500–599 Jewish Literature

500 Jewish Literature—History and Development
530 Jewish Literature—Criticism and Analysis
540 Jewish Literature—Study and Teaching
550 Jewish Literature—Anthologies and Selections
560 Jewish Literature—Individual Works
590 General Literature Related to Jews and Judaism

600–699 The Jewish Community: Society and the Arts

600 Jewish Social Institutions and Behavior
610 Personal and Social Customs

620 Jewish Community Structure and Governance
635 Communal Institutions and Organizations
645 Jewish Economic Institutions and Behavior
650 Social Conditions and Problems
660 The Jews in the World Order
670 Jewish Graphic and Plastic Arts
685 Jewish Music
690 Public Entertainment, Mass Media
699 Cooking and Culinary Arts

700–799 Jewish History, Geography, Biography

700 Jewish History
710 The Emergence of the Jewish People (20th–5th Centuries BCE)
720 The Emergence of Talmudic Judaism (5th Century BCE–8th Century CE)
730 The Era of Normative Judaism (9th–19th Centuries)
735 The Contemporary Era (20th Century–)
740 The Jews of the Middle East
750 Sephardic and Mediterranean Jewry
760 Ashkenazic and Eastern European Jewry
765 Western European Jewry
770 United States Jewry
785 South American Jewry
790 African Jewry
795 Geography
799 Collective Biography

800–899 Israel and Zionism

800	Zionism
805	National Institutions, Zionist Organizational Structure
810	Zionist Parties and Popular Organizations
820	Israel (*Eretz Yisrael*)
830	Israel—Geography
840	Israel—Government and Politics
855	Israel—Economics and Development
865	Israel—Demography, Population
875	Israel—Culture
880	Israel—Arts
885	Israel and World Jewry
890	Israel and the Middle East

900–999 General Works

900	Jewish Encyclopedias
910	General Collections of Essays
915	Jewish Yearbooks, Almanacs, Directories
920	Jewish Journalism
940	The Jewish Book
950	Jewish Bibliography
960	Audiovisual Materials
970	Library Science
980	The Jewish Library
995	The Jewish Museum

001–099

Bible and Biblical Studies

001 **Complete Bible**
    Includes only the Jewish *Tanakh*.
    For the Christian Scriptures "New Testament," see 292.1

.1   Art, Rare and Special Editions
.2   Hebrew with Translation
    e.g., Hebrew to English
    For the history of biblical translation, see 003.8
.5   Polyglot Bibles
    More than two languages
.8   Combined "Old Testament" and "New Testament"
    For Christian Scriptures as an individual work, see 292.1

002 **Bible Commentaries—Classical**
    Including Bibles with textual interpretation, e.g., Rashi, Ibn Ezra, *Mikra'ot Gedolot*

> For Bible criticism, see 005; for non-Jewish commentaries, see 002.8

.1 Commentaries in the Traditional Vein—Non-Classical
.2 Current Basic Commentaries
> e.g., Soncino, S.L. Gordon
.3 Scientific Approach and Interpretation
> e.g., Cassuto
.7 History of Biblical Commentary
> Works about individual commentators may be put with their respective works
.8 Non-Jewish Commentaries
> e.g., Anchor Bible, Interpreter's Bible

003 Aids for the Study of the Bible
.1 Outlines
.2 Study Guides and Introductions
.3 Study and Teaching
> For the teaching of the Bible in elementary and secondary schools, see 346 and 356, respectively
.35 Textbooks
.4 Dictionaries
> Including encyclopedic dictionaries
> For language dictionaries, see 004.4
.5 Concordances
.6 Indexes
.7 History of the Bible
.8 History of Biblical Translations
.9 Biblical Abridgements and Selections

004 Biblical Linguistics
.1 Etymology, Derivation, Semantics
.2 Orthography and Alphabets

.3	Study and Teaching
.4	Language Dictionaries
.5	Synonyms and Homonyms
.6	Phonology, Phonetics, Pronunciation
.7	Prosody
.8	Grammar

005 Bible—Research and Criticism
e.g., Works of Wellhausen and Kaufman

.8 Non-Jewish Orientation
Including material specifically non-Jewish in approach, as well as by non-Jews

006 Biblical Institutions and Society

.1	Political Life and Institutions
.11	Tribes and Tribal System
.12	Monarchy
.2	Social Life and Institutions
.21	Family
.22	Women
	For biography, see 008
.3	Religious Life and Institutions
.31	Sacrifices (*Korban*)
.32	Priesthood, Priestly Office (*Kohen, Kohanim*)
.33	Levites, Levitical Office (*Levi, Levi'im*)
.4	Military Institutions, Warfare
.5	Ark of the Covenant (*Aron Ha-brit*)
.6	Tabernacle (*Mishkan*)
.7	Temple (*Bet ha-Mikdash*)
	For material on the historical period, see 716–727
.71	First Temple
.72	Second Temple

007   Biblical History
   Including material directly related to the Bible and life in biblical times
   For other related material see history, 700–729, and 090 for Ancient Near Eastern Civilizations
  .1   Patriarchal. 20th–14th Centuries BCE
  .2   Exodus. 14th–13th Centuries BCE
  .3   Conquest and Judges. 13th Century to 1004 BCE
  .4   United Kingdom. 1004–928 BCE
  .5   Israel and Judah. 928–586 BCE
  .6   Babylonian Exile. 586–538 BCE
  .7   Second Commonwealth. 538 BCE–70 CE
       As relates to biblical history only

008   Biblical Biography
  .2   Fictional Reconstructions; Personalities
  .3   Bible Stories—Collections

009   The Biblical Environment
       For archeology see 010
  .1   Geography
       Including atlases
  .2   Geology
  .3   Botany
  .4   Zoology
  .5   Ecology

010   Biblical Archeology
       Including archeology dealing directly with the biblical environment
       For related archeological materials, see 090–099 and 820.5
  .5   Dead Sea Scrolls

.8	Archeological Sites
.9	Antiquities

011 Contents of the Bible
.1   Bible as Law
.2   Bible as Religious Thought and Philosophy
.3   Bible as an Educational Tool
.5   Bible as Literature
.6   Bible as Political Thought
.7   Bible as History

012 Special Topics
.1   Medicine
.2   Astronomy; Astrology
.3   Technology
.4   Mathematics

013 The Impact of the Bible
.1   Impact on non-Jewish Religions
.2   Impact on Social Movements
.3   Impact on Literature
.4   Impact on Law
.5   Impact on Political Thought
.6   Impact on Western Civilization
.7   Impact on American Civilization
.8   Impact on Eastern Civilization

014 Essays on the Bible
    Including theoretical, philosophic, sermonic
.1   Sermons of the Bible
.5   Philosophic Essays
.9   Pseudo-Research of the Bible
    Including frauds, forgeries

015 Torah (Pentateuch, Five Books of Moses)

Including editions with *Haftarot* and works dealing with the portion of the week

- .1 Art, Rare and Special Editions
- .2 Hebrew with Translation
  See note under 001.2
- .5 Polyglot
  See note under 001.5
- .9 Abridgements
- .91 Stories on the *Sedarot*

016 Commentaries on the Torah—Classic

See note under 002

- .1 Commentaries in the Traditional Vein—Non-Classical
  e.g., Leibowitz, Zornberg
- .2 Current Basic Commentaries
- .3 Scientific Approach and Interpretation
- .7 History of Torah Commentary
- .8 Non-Jewish Commentaries

017 Aids for the Study of the Torah

- .1 Outlines
- .2 Study Guides and Introductions
- .3 Study and Teaching
  See note under 003.3
- .35 Textbooks
- .4 Dictionaries
- .5 Concordances
- .6 Indexes

.9	Preparation of the Scrolls e.g., scribes, writing
018	Torah—Research and Criticism See note under 005
019	Contents of the Torah
.1	Torah as Law
.2	Torah as Religious Thought and Philosophy
.3	Torah as an Educational Tool
.6	Torah as Political Thought
.7	Torah as History
.9	Special Topics Divide like 012
020	Genesis (*Bereshit*)
.09	Abridgements
.1	Art, Rare and Special Editions
.2	Commentaries—Classic
.21	Commentaries in the Traditional Vein—Non-Classical
.22	Current Basic Commentaries
.23	Scientific Approach and Interpretation
.28	Non-Jewish Commentaries
.3	Study and Teaching
.5	Research and Criticism
.7	Environment See 009
.8	Personalities
.9	Special topics

021		Exodus (*Shemot*) Including *Aseret Ha-Dibbrot* (Ten Commandments) Divide like 020
022		Leviticus (*Va-Yikra*) Divide like 020
023		Numbers (*Ba-Midbar*) Divide like 020
024		Deuteronomy (*Devarim*) Divide like 020
025		*Nevi'im* (**Prophets**) Divide like 015
026		Commentaries on *Nevi'im* (Classical) Divide like 016
027		Aids for the Study of *Nevi'im* Divide like 017
	.8	Research and Criticism
	.88	Non-Jewish Orientation
	.9	Special Topics See 012
028		Joshua (*Yehoshua*) Divide like 020
029		Judges (*Shoftim*) Divide like 020

030	**I Samuel** (*Shemuel Alef*) Including books combining I and II Samuel *Divide like 020*
031	**II Samuel** (*Shemuel Bet*) *Divide like 020*
032	**I Kings** (*Melakhim Alef*) Including books combining I and II Kings *Divide like 020*
033	**II Kings** (*Melakhim Bet*) *Divide like 020*
034	**Isaiah** (*Yeshayahu*) *Divide like 020*
035	**Jeremiah** (*Yirmeyahu*) *Divide like 020*
036	**Ezekiel** (*Yehezkel*) *Divide like 020*
037	**Twelve Prophets** (*Tere Asar*) *Divide like 020*
038	**Hosea** (*Hoshea*) *Divide like 020*
039	**Joel** (*Yoel*) *Divide like 020*

040 Amos (*Amos*)
      Divide like 020

041 Obadiah (*Ovadyah*)
      Divide like 020

042 Jonah (*Yonah*)
      Divide like 020

043 Micah (*Mikhah*)
      Divide like 020

044 Nahum (*Nahum*)
      Divide like 020

045 Habakuk (*Habakuk*)
      Divide like 020

046 Zephaniah (*Zephanyah*)
      Divide like 020

047 Haggai (*Hagai*)
      Divide like 020

048 Zechariah (*Zekharyah*)
      Divide like 020

049 Malachi (*Malakhi*)
      Divide like 020

050 Ketuvim (Writings)
      Divide like 015

051	Commentaries on *Ketuvim*—Classic *Divide like 016 where applicable*
052	Aids to the Study of *Ketuvim* *Divide like 017*
053	Research and Criticism
054	Special Topics *See 012*
055 .2 .7	Wisdom Literature Wisdom Literature as Religious Thought History
056	Psalms (*Tehillim*) *Divide like 020*
057	Proverbs (*Mishle*) *Divide like 020*
058	Job (*Iyov*) *Divide like 020*
059	Five Megilloth (*Hamesh Megillot*) *Divide like 020*
060	Song of Songs (*Shir ha-Shirim*) *Divide like 020*
061	Ruth (*Rut*) *Divide like 020*

062	Lamentations (*Aykha*)
	Divide like 020

063	Ecclesiastes (*Kohelet*)
	Divide like 020

064	Esther (*Megilat Ester*)
	Divide like 020

065	Daniel (*Daniel*)
	Divide like 020

066	Ezra (*Ezra*)
	Divide like 020

067	Nehemiah (*Nehemyah*)
	Divide like 020

068	I Chronicles (*Divrei ha-Yamim Alef*)
	Including books combining I and II Chronicles
	Divide like 020

069	II Chronicles (*Divrei ha-Yamim Bet*)
	Divide like 020

070 Apocrypha
.09	Abridgements
.1	Art, Rare and Special Editions
.2	Traditional Commentaries
.3	Introductions, Study Guides
.4	Dictionaries, Concordances
.5	Modern Criticism and Interpretation

	.7	Environment of Apocryphal Books *See* 009
	.8	Contents *See* 011
	.9	Special Topics *See* 012
071		I and II Esdras
072		Tobit
073		Judith
074		Esther, Additions; Wisdom of Solomon
075		Ecclesiastes (Wisdom of Ben Sira)
076		Baruch; Epistle of Jeremy
077		The Song of the Three Children; Susanna; Bel and the Dragon; The Prayer of Manasseh
078		I Maccabees
079		II Maccabees

080 *Pseudepigrapha*
Divide like 070

081   Palestinian Pseudepigrapha

082	Legends about Biblical Characters
.1	The Testaments of the Twelve Patriarchs
.2	The Book of Jubilees
.3	The Martyrdom of Isaiah
.4	Epistle of Jeremiah; Chronicles of Jeremiah
.5	The Lives of the Prophets
.6	The Testament of Job
.7	The Life of Adam and Eve

083	Hymns and Psalms
.1	The Cantica
.2	The Psalms of Solomon

084	Apocalypses
.1	The Book of Enoch
.2	The Assumption of Moses
.3	The Apocalypse of Baruch

085	Alexandrian Pseudepigrapha
.1	The Letter of Aristeas
.2	The Sibylline Oracles

086	III Maccabees

087	IV Maccabees

088	Apocalypses of Alexandrian Pseudepigrapha
.1	Slavonic Enoch
.2	Greek Baruch

090 Ancient Near East (sometimes designated Middle East, West Asia, or Fertile Crescent)

Including material elucidating the ancient Near Eastern background and setting in which the Bible emerged

091 Archeology of the Ancient Near East

For biblical archeology see 010; for post-biblical archeology, e.g., Bar Kochba, Masada, see respective section in the 820s

092 Ancient Near Eastern Religions
- .1 Myth and Mythology
- .9 Research

093 The Civilization of Egypt
- .1 Law
- .2 Mythology and Religion
- .4 Economics and Commerce
- .5 Political Organization
- .6 Social Organization
- .7 History
- .71 Kingdoms of Upper and Lower Egypt (BCE 2700)
- .72 Old Kingdom (BCE 2700–2200)
- .73 Middle Kingdom (BCE 2000–1546)
- .74 New Kingdom (BCE 1546–1200)
- .75 BCE (1200–525)
- .76 Persian and Hellenistic Egypt (BCE 525–30)
- .9 Research

  Including Egyptology

094 The Civilization of Mesopotamia and the Northern Fertile Crescent
Divide like 093.1–.7
- .7 History
- .71 Sumerian City-States (BCE 2000)
- .72 Akkadian Civilization
- .73 Old Babylonia (BCE 2000-1300)
- .74 Assyria (BCE 1950-625)
- .75 Neo-Babylonia (BCE 625-539)
- .9 Research
  Including Assyriology

095 The Civilization of Canaan and Transjordan
Divide like 093.1–.7
- .7 History
- .71 Canaanites
- .72 Phoenicians
- .73 Arameans (Syrians)
- .74 Moabites
- .75 Desert Tribes

096 Asia Minor and the Mediterranean World
Divide like 093.1–.1
- .7 History
- .71 Hittites (BCE 720)
- .72 Seleucid Empire (BCE 333-64)
- .73 Greece

097 Persia
Divide like 093.1–.7

100–199

Classical Judaica: Halakhah and Midrash

100 *Jewish Law, Lore, and Thought*
General works encompassing the entire field of Jewish law, lore, or thought, including histories, essays, and critical discussions
.2   Addresses, Essays, and Lectures
.3   Study and Teaching
.4   Encyclopedias
.5   Anthologies
.9   Special Topics

101 *Talmud with Traditional Commentaries*
Including Babylonian Talmud with standard commentaries
For Jerusalem Talmud, see 115

.1 Special Editions
    Including translations of the Talmud published without commentaries
.2 Abridgements, Anthologies, Selections
.3 Classical Commentaries
    Including commentaries published separately from standard editions of Talmud, or individual commentaries, e.g., Rashi and works about specific commentaries of commentators
.4 Current Basic Commentaries
    e.g., Soncino and Steinsaltz with commentary and translation
.5 Commentaries in the Traditional Vein—Non-Classical
    e.g., Art Scroll
.6 *Hiddushim* (Novellae)
    Commentaries on the Talmud and later rabbinic works that attempt to derive new facts or principles from the implications of the text
.7 History of Talmudic Commentary
.8 Non-Jewish Commentaries
.9 Special Topics
    e.g., *Gematria*, sacrifices, women

102 Aids for the Study of the Talmud
.1 Outlines, Contents, Introductions
.2 Study Guides
.3 Study and Teaching of the Talmud
.35 Textbooks
.4 Talmudic Language
    Including idioms and abbreviations
.5 Dictionaries

.6	Concordances
.7	Talmudic Method and System
	Examinations of the methods of Talmudic logic and systemization

103 Research and Critical Studies

.1	General Works on the Talmud
.2	Apologetics
.3	Textual Criticism
.5	Talmudic Thought
.6	Talmudic Science
.7	History and Development
	Including biographical material and life in Talmudic times

104 Zera'im

Major numbers indicate *Seder* (Order) followed by the tractates (i.e., *Berakhote, Pe'ah*) within the *Seder*. Materials dealing with the *Seder* as a whole are to be classified under the *Seder* number (except Study and Teaching in 102.3).

.01	Introductions and Outlines
.02	Commentaries
.05	*Hiddushim*
.06	Research and Criticism
.A	*Berakhot*
.A1	Introductions and Outlines
.A2	Commentaries
.A5	*Hiddushim*
.B	*Pe'ah*
	Divide like 104.A

50 A CLASSIFICATION SYSTEM FOR LIBRARIES OF JUDAICA

    .C   *Demai*
            Divide like 104.A
    .D   *Kilayim*
            Divide like 104.A
    .E   *Shevi'it*
            Divide like 104.A
    .F   *Terumot*
            Divide like 104.A
    .G   *Ma'aserot*
            Divide like 104.A
    .H   *Ma'aser Sheni*
            Divide like 104.A
    .I   *Hallah*
            Divide like 104.A
    .J   *Orlah*
            Divide like 104.A
    .K   *Bikkurim*
            Divide like 104.A

105   **Mo'ed**
            Divide like 104, e.g., 105.01
    .A   *Shabbat*
            Divide like 104.A
    .B   *Eruvin*
            Divide like 104.A
    .C   *Pesahim*
            Divide like 104.A
    .D   *Shekalim*
            Divide like 104.A
    .E   *Yoma*
            Divide like 104.A
    .F   *Sukkah*
            Divide like 104.A

100–199

- .G **Betzah**
  Divide like 104.A
- .H **Rosh Ha-Shanah**
  Divide like 104.A
- .I **Ta'anit**
  Divide like 104.A
- .J **Megillah**
  Divide like 104.A
- .K **Mo'ed Katan**
  Divide like 104.A
- .L **Hagigah**
  Divide like 104.A

106 Nashim
Divide like 104, e.g., 106.01

- .A **Yevamot**
  Divide like 104.A
- .B **Ketubbot**
  Divide like 104.A
- .C **Nedarim**
  Divide like 104.A
- .D **Nazir**
  Divide like 104.A
- .E **Sotah**
  Divide like 104.A
- .F **Gittin**
  Divide like 104.A
- .G **Kiddushin**
  Divide like 104.A

107 Nezikin
Divide like 104, e.g., 107.01

.A Bava Kamma
    Divide like 104.A
.B Bava Mezia
    Divide like 104.A
.C Bava Batra
    Divide like 104.A
.D Sanhedrin
    Divide like 104.A
.E Makkot
    Divide like 104.A
.F Shevu'ot
    Divide like 104.A
.G Eduyyot
    Divide like 104.A
.H Avodah Zarah
    Divide like 104.A
.I Avot
    Divide like 104.A
    .12   Pirkei Avot (Ethics of the Fathers)
.J Horayot
    Divide like 104.A

108 **Kodashim**
    Divide like 104, e.g., 108.01
.A Zevahim
    Divide like 104.A
.B Menahot
    Divide like 104.A
.C Hullin
    Divide like 104.A
.D Bekhorot
    Divide like 104.A

.E   **Arakhin**
        Divide like 104.A
.F   **Temurah**
        Divide like 104.A
.G   **Keritot**
        Divide like 104.A
.H   **Me'ilah**
        Divide like 104.A
.I   **Tamid**
        Divide like 104.A
.J   **Middot**
        Divide like 104.A
.K   **Kinnim**
        Divide like 104.A

109   **Tohorot**
        Divide like 104, e.g., 109.01
.A   **Kelim**
        Divide like 104.A
.B   **Oholot**
        Divide like 104.A
.C   **Nega'im**
        Divide like 104.A
.D   **Parah**
        Divide like 104.A
.E   **Tohorot**
        Divide like 104.A
.F   **Mikva'ot**
        Divide like 104.A
.G   **Niddah**
        Divide like 104.A
.H   **Makhshirin**
        Divide like 104.A

.I   Zavim
         Divide like 104.A
.J   Tevul Yom
         Divide like 104.A
.K   Yadayim
         Divide like 104.A
.L   Ukzin
         Divide like 104.A

110   Mishnah
.1   Special Editions
.2   Traditional Commentaries
.21   Modern Commentaries
.3   Zera'im
         Divide like 104.A
.4   Mo'ed
         Divide like 104.A
.5   Nashim
         Divide like 104.A
.6   Nezikim
         Divide like 104.A
.7   Kodashim
         Divide like 104.A
.8   Tohorot
         Divide like 104.A
.9   Anthologies and Abridgements

111   Mishnah, Works on
.3   Study and Teaching
.35   Textbooks
.4   Dictionaries, Concordances
.6   Research and Critical Studies

	.7	History and Development of the *Mishnah* Including *Zugot* and *Tannaim*
	.8	Mishnaic Method and System
	.9	Special Topics
112		Halakhah in the Mishnaic Period
113		Baraita
114		Halakhic *Midrashim*
	.1	*Mekhilta* (on The Book of Exodus)
	.2	*Sifra* (on The Book of Leviticus)
	.3	*Sifrei* (on The Books of Numbers and Deuteronomy)
115		*Jerusalem Talmud (Talmud Yerushalmi)*
	.1	Special Editions
	.2	Traditional Commentaries
	.3	*Zera'im*
	.4	*Mo'ed*
	.5	*Nashim*
	.6	*Nezikin*
	.7	*Niddah*
	.9	Anthologies and Abridgements
116		Jerusalem Talmud, Works on
	.3	Study and Teaching
	.35	Textbooks
	.4	Dictionaries, Concordances
	.6	Research and Critical Studies
	.7	History and Development
	.9	Special Topics

120 History and Development of the Gemara
Including Amoraim

121 Tosefta
.6   Research and Critical Studies

123 Extra-Canonical Talmudic Tractates
.1   *Avot de-Rabbi Nathan*
.2   *Soferim*
.3   *Evel Rabbati*
.4   *Kallah*
.5   *Derekh Eretz Rabbah*
.6   *Derekh Eretz Zuta*
.7   *Perek Ha-Shalom*
.9   Other Small Tractates

124 The Impact of the Talmud
Divide like 013

125 Post-Talmudic Halakhah
Commentaries on and additions to the system of Jewish law in the Talmud and basic to normative Jewish law after the completion of the Gemara

.1   *Taryag Mitzvot* (613 Commandments)
.4   Codes
        Logically ordered books of law codifying the Talmud and later decisions. Including only general works on codes
        For specific codes, see subsequent numbers, e.g., Mishneh Torah, **128**

.5	Responsa
	Written replies given to questions on all aspects of Jewish law by qualified authorities from the time of the later *Geonim* to the present day. Including only general works on the responsa
	For responsa of specific individuals and periods see appropriate period classification below
.6	Research and Critical Studies
.7	History and Development
.9	Special Topics

126 *Geonim*
Babylonian scholars and intellectual leaders from sixth through eleventh centuries; including *Saboraim*

.4	Codes
.5	Responsa
.6	Research and Criticism
.7	History and Development

127 *Rishonim*
Talmudic commentaries and codifiers of the period from the eleventh century to the compilations of the *Shulhan Arukh* in 1565

.3	*Tosafot*
.4	Codes
	For Mishneh Torah, see **128**; Shulhan Arukh, see **129**
.41	Abridgements of the text
.5	Responsa
.6	Research and Critical Studies
.7	History and Development

128 Mishneh Torah

> For separate editions of individual books of the Mishneh Torah use two decimal places, e.g., Book of Cleanliness 128.01

- .1 Special Editions
- .2 Traditional Commentaries
- .3 Study and Teaching
- .35 Textbooks
- .4 Outlines, Introductions, and Study Guides
- .5 Abridgements
- .6 Research and Criticism
- .8 Method and System
- .9 Special Topics

129 Shulhan Arukh

- .1 Special Editions
- .2 Traditional Commentaries
- .3 Study and Teaching
- .4 Research and Criticism
- .5 Abridgements
  Including *Kitzur Shulhan Arukh*
- .6 *Orah Hayyim*
- .7 *Yoreh De'ah*
- .8 *Even ha-Ezer*
- .9 *Hoshen Mishpat*

130 Aharonim

> Rabbinic authorities from the sixteenth through nineteenth centuries
> *Divide like 127*

131	**Contemporary Jewish Law**
	Divide like 127
.5	Responsa
.51	Orthodox
.52	Traditional (The Movement)
	e.g., Union for Traditional Judaism
.53	Conservative
.54	Reform
.55	Reconstructionist

134 Comparative Law

135 Jewish Thought—General Works

Including Midrash and Aggadah (the stories, sayings, and moral teachings of the Oral Law); Kabbalah (Jewish mysticism or theosophy); and Jewish philosophy

.1	Special Editions
.2	Outlines, Introductions
.3	Study and Teaching
.35	Textbooks
.4	Dictionaries, Encyclopedias
.5	Anthologies, Selections
.6	Research and Criticism
.7	History
.8	Methodology, Logic

136 Jewish Theological and Theosophic Concepts

Including material that deals with general concepts. Material on specific value concepts should be classified under the appropriate category (e.g., material concerning *tzedakah* under 136.4, justice). Each category also includes material about concepts expressing directly opposing ideas (e.g., material on idolatry under 136.3, Kingship of God)

.1 Nature and Attributes of God (*Ma'aseh Merkavah*)
.11 Holiness (*Kedushah*)
.12 Appelatives for God
.13 Revelation of God (*Gilluy Shekhinah*)
    For revelation of His personality and power. For revelation of His law or commandments, see 136.31
.14 Omnipotence
.15 Omniscience
.16 Immanence
.18 Anthropomorphism
.2 Metaphysics and Cosmology
.21 Creation and the Natural Order
.22 Miracles (*Nissim*)
.25 *Olam* (Time, Space, and Eternity)
.29 Evil
.3 Fear of God (*Yirat Shamayim*)
.31 God's Covenant (*Brit*)
.32 Faith and Trust in God (*Emunah, Bittahon*)
.37 Creeds, Articles of Faith
.38 Agnosticism (*Apikoros*)
.39 Idolatry (*Avodah Zarah*); Atheism
.4 Justice (*Tzedakah*)
.41 Law
.42 The Political Order
    Including materials on Jewish political thought. For Jewish communal government, see 620; for behavior of Jews in general political situations, see 668

.48	Chastisements (*Yissurin*)
.5	God's Love and Mercy (*Hesed/Middah Ha-Rahamim*)
.51	Hesed (Covenant Love)
.52	*Gemilut Hasadim*
.53	Imitation of God
.55	Prayer (*Tefilah*)
	For liturgy, see 230
.56	Repentance (*Teshuvah*)
.57	Atonement (*Kapparot*)
.6	Torah
	Works on the religious and spiritual impact of the Torah as a means of experiencing God
	For works dealing with the Torah [The Five Books of Moses] see 016
.61	Giving of the Torah (*Mattan Torah*)
.65	Study and Learning
	As a concept
.69	Ignorance and the Ignorant
.7	*Mitzvot* (Commandments)
.71	Sanctification of God's Name (*Kiddush ha-Shem*)
.75	Ethics (*Derekh Eretz*)
	Practical discussions of specific ethical problems can be classified with their respective subjects, e.g., ethics of marriage, 652
.78	Sin
.79	Profanation of God's Name (*Hillul ha-Shem*)
.8	The People of Israel (*Am Yisrael*)
.81	Election of Israel (Chosen People)
.85	Land of Israel (*Eretz Yisrael*)
.88	God, Israel, and "The Nations"
	e.g., Noachide Laws
.9	Messianism and Eschatology

.91   End of Days (*Aharit ha-Yamim*)
.92   Messianic Era
.93   Hereafter, World to Come (*Olam ha-Ba*)
.94   Resurrection

140   Aggadah—Classical Midrash

Rabbinic books written from Tannaitic times to the tenth century containing non-Halakhic biblical interpretations in the spirit of the Aggudah
Divide like 135; for folklore, see 185

141   Biblical Midrashim

Including general works about and collections of

.1   **Midrash Rabbah**
.11   Genesis (*Bereshit*) *Rabbah*
.12   Exodus (*Shemot*) *Rabbah*
.13   Leviticus (*Va-Yikrah*) *Rabbah*
.14   Numbers (*Bamidbar*) *Rabbah*
.15   Deuteronomy (*Devarim*) *Rabbah*
.2   Five Megilloth (*Hamesh Megillot*) *Rabbah*
.21   Song of Songs (*Shir Ha-shirim*) *Rabbah*
.22   Ruth (*Rut*) *Rabbah*
.23   Lamentations (*Kinot*) *Rabbah*
.24   Ecclesiastes (*Kohelet*) *Rabbah*
.25   Esther (*Ester*) *Rabbah*

142   Ethical *Midrashim*

143   Festival *Midrashim* (*Pesiktot*)

| 144 | Historical *Midrashim* |

145	Post-Classical *Midrashim* and Midrashic Collection
.5	Ein Ya'akov
.6	Modern *Midrashim*

150 Kabbalah
Divide like 135
| .9 | Special Topics |
| | e.g., *Tzimtzum* |

151	Theoretical Kabbalah
	e.g., Theories of Emanation, *Sefirot*
.5	*Sefer Yetzirah*

152	Practical Kabbalah
.1	Theurgic Kabbalah
.2	*Gematria*

153	Pre-Classical Kabbalah
	Talmudic period and earlier
.1	*Ma'aseh Bereshit*
	Speculations on Creation, Cosmology
.2	*Ma'aseh Merkavah*
	Speculations on the Nature of God

| 154 | Jewish Gnosticism |

155	Geonic Kabbalah
.1	*Hekhalot* Literature
.2	*Shi'ur Komah*

156   German Kabbalah
  .1   Hymns of Glory (*Shir ha-Kavod*)

157   Prophetic (Abulafian) Kabbalah
       Divide like 135

158   Classical (Sephardic) Kabbalah
       Divide like 135

159   Zohar
       Divide like 135

160   Palestinian Kabbalah
  .1   Cordovero and his System
  .2   Luria and his System
  .3   Shabbatean Kabbalah

161   Hasidic Kabbalah
       Including material on hasidic thought but not on the sociology of the *Hasidim*
       Divide like 135. For other material on Hasidism, see 213

162   Modern Kabbalah
  .5   Kook and his System

163   Jewish Kabbalistic Heresies
       Excluding Gnosticism

164   Non-Jewish Kabbalistic Adaptations
  .1   Gnosticism
  .2   Christian Kabbalah
  .3   Free Masonry

.4	Secularized Kabbalistic Ideas Including relevant materials of or on Spinoza and Freud
.5	Magic and Alchemy
.9	Comparative Mysticism
165	**Hellenistic Jewish Thought** Divide like 136. For Hellenism, see 660.2
.8	Philo

170 Medieval Jewish Thought
Divide like 136

171	Saadiah Gaon Including biographical material
172	Judah Halevi Including biographical material
173	Maimonides Including biographical material For *Mishneh Torah*, see 128; for *Sepher ha-Ma'or,* see 110.2
.1	*Shemonah Perakim*
.2	*Thirteen Articles of Faith*
.3	*Guide of the Perplexed*
.4	*Sefer ha-Mitzvot*
.5	*Other works*
174	**Other Medieval Jewish Philosophers**

175 Modern Jewish Thought
Where applicable, divide like 136. For specifically Zionist thought, see 802

176 Liberalism and Reform
e.g., Mendelsohn, Kuhler

177 Idealism
e.g., Krochmal, Hermann Cohen

178 Non-Orthodox Traditionalism, Historical School
Including Conservative or Masorati Jewish thought. For Conservative movement, see 215; for Jewish law, see 131.53

179 Orthodoxy, Neo-Orthodoxy
e.g., Samson Raphael Hirsch

180 Jewish Existentialism
e.g., Franz Rosenzweig, Martin Buber

181 Religious Naturalism
e.g., Mordacai M. Kaplan, Reconstructionist thought
- .1 Reconstructionism
- .2 Humanistic Judaism

182 Non-Kabbalistic Mysticism
e.g., Heschel

183 Secularism

| 184 | Comparative Philosophy |

185	*Jewish Folklore*
	For Rabbinical Aggadah, see 140
.3	Study and Teaching
.5	Research and Criticism
.6	Anthologies
.7	History

| 186 | Proverbs, Folk Expressions |
| | General works only |

| 187 | Folklore on Biblical Themes |
| .5 | Ten Lost Tribes |

| 188 | Folklore on Talmudic Themes |

| 189 | Sephardic Folklore |

190	Ashkenazic Folklore
.3	Chelm Stories
.5	Hasidic Folklore

| 191 | Oriental Jewish Folklore |

| 192 | Western European Jewish Folklore |

| 193 | Jewish Folklore of the Americas |

| 194 | Folklore of the Land of Israel |

195   Folklore Concerning the Jews
            Including legends of the Wandering Jew
    .1   Christian Folklore
    .2   Moslem and Arabic Folklore

196   Comparative Folklore
    .4   Encyclopedias and Dictionaries
    .5   Research and History
    .6   Selections; Anthologies

200-299

Jewish Observance and Practice

200 **Jewish Religion—General Works**
  Including introductions to the Jewish religion
 .3 Addresses, Essays, and Lectures

202 Homiletics, Sermonic Material
 .1 Shabbat
 .2 Festivals
 .3 Confirmation and Graduation
 .4 Marriage
 .5 Funeral
 .6 Political and Patriotic
 .7 Other Occasions

203 Study and Teaching
  For elementary education, see **347**; *for secondary education, see* **357**
 .05 Quiz Books

.8 Conversion to Judaism
Including texts for converts
For history of Conversion, see 207.9
.85 Personal narratives of converts

204 Dictionaries and Encyclopedias

205 Yearbooks

206 Research and Criticism

207 History of the Jewish Religion
For history of the Jewish people, see the 700s
.1 Patriarchal Period (20th–14th Centuries BCE)
.2 The First Commonwealth (13th–14th Centuries BCE)
.3 Epoch of Talmudic Judaism (5th Century BCE–8th Century CE)
.4 Epoch of Normative Judaism (9th–19th Centuries CE)
.5 Contemporary Epoch (20th Century–)
.8 Messianic Movements
e.g., Shabbateans
.9 Conversions
For teaching of converts, see 203.8

210 *Jewish Religious Movements*
Only includes general materials on Jewish religious movements presently in existence
For materials on defunct religious movements, e.g., Pharisees, see classifications for their respective historical periods. For material on indi-

vidual movements now in existence see respective numbers below

211	Samaritans
212	Karaism, Karaite Sect
213	Hasidism, Hasidic Movements
	For Hasidic thought, see 161; for Hasidic folklore, see 190.5
.9	Anti-Hasidic Writings
214	Orthodoxy
	For Orthodox thought, see 179
.5	Ba'alei Teshuvah Movement
215	Conservatism
	For Conservative thought, see 178
216	Reconstructionism
	For Reconstructionist thought, see 181
217	Reform and Liberal Movements
	For Reform and Liberal thought, see 176
219	Other Religious Movements
	e.g., Jewish Science

220 Guides to Jewish Living—General Works

Includes rabbinical counseling. For counseling not related to Jewish subjects, see the 390s

221   Laws (*Halakhot*), Customs, and Ceremonies
            Including those that are practiced on a regular and continuing basis throughout the life of a Jew
   .1   *Kashrut* (Dietary Laws)
   .2   *Tefillin* (Phylacteries)
   .3   *Tzitzit; Tallit*
   .5   *Mikveh* (Ritual bath); *Taharat Ha-Mishpahah* (Laws of family purity)
            For construction of mikvaot, see 673.6

222   Rites of Jewish Personal Living
            Including rites of passage occurring once in a lifetime
   .1   *Brit Milah* (Circumcision)
   .11   Names and Naming
            Including name books and naming ceremonies
   .2   *Pidyon ha-Ben* (Redemption of the First Born)
   .3   Bar Mitzvah
   .31   Bat Mitzvah
   .4   Marriage and Divorce
   .5   Death and Mourning
            Including customs of death, anniversaries, and commemorations, e.g., *Yahrzeit*

223   Jewish Home Observances
            Excluding those connected with Shabbat and holidays
   .1   *Hanukkat Habayit* (Dedication of a new home)
            Including *Mezuzah*

224   Synagogue
            Including only observance, practices, and rites
            For history, see 636

.1	*Kriat Ha-Torah* (Reading from the Torah)
.2	*Haftarot* (Reading from the Prophets)
	See also 025
.3	*Minyan* (Quorum for conducting public worship)
.9	Contemporary Synagogue Rites
.91	Confirmation

225 Jewish Symbols
For symbols associated with specific holidays, see holiday

.1	*Kipah* (*Yarmulke*)
.2	Menorah
	For Hanukkah "menorah" see 247.1
.3	*Magen David* (Star of David)

230 *Jewish Liturgy*

Including general works dealing with liturgy and the service. Specific works, *siddurim, mahzorim*, etc., go either under Sephardic or Ashkenazic liturgy or under its respective holiday, e.g., Shabbat, Rosh Ha-Shanah, etc.
For works dealing with the concept and purposes of prayer, see 136.55

.3	Study and Teaching
	For elementary education, see 347; for secondary education, see 357
.4	Encyclopedias
.5	Introductions and Study Guides
.7	History and Development
.8	*Piyyutim* (Hebrew liturgical poems)
.9	Prayers for Special Occasions
.91	*Berakhot* (Blessings)
.92	*Birkat Ha-mazon* (Blessing after meals)

231	Sephardic Liturgy (Including Oriental and Yemenite)
	All liturgy except that which deals specifically with Shabbat and festivals
.1	*Siddurim* (Prayer books)
	See note above
.2	Commentaries
.3	Study and Teaching
.4	Encyclopedias
.5	Abridgements, Anthologies, Selections
.6	Research and Criticism
.7	History and Development

232	Ashkenazic Liturgy
	Divide like 231

233	Liturgy of Other Communities
	Divide like 740–794

234	Supplemental, Non-Traditional, and Modern Liturgies
.1	Reform
.2	Reconstructionist
.3	Non-Traditional Conservative
	For traditional Conservative liturgy, see 232

235 *The Jewish Calendar*
.1	Comprehensive Calendars
.2	Sabbatical and Jubilee Years
.7	History of Jewish Calendar

236		**Holidays, Festivals, Observances**
		General information about the holidays including history, laws, customs and ceremonies, etc.
		For individual holidays, see 237–265
	.1	Laws, Customs, and Ceremonies
		Including symbols
	.2	Liturgy
	.3	Study and Teaching
	.4	Dictionaries
	.5	Literature
		Works, including stories, explicitly pertaining to holidays and festivals
		Divide like 500
	.6	Program Material, Arts and Crafts, Music and Song
	.7	History and Development
	.85	Folklore
237		**Shabbat (Sabbath)**
	.1	Laws, Customs, and Ceremonies
	.11	*Kabbalat Shabbat* (Welcoming of the Sabbath)
	.12	*Kiddush* (Blessing over the wine)
	.13	*Se'udah Shelishit* (Third meal)
	.14	*Havdalah* (Ceremony marking the end of the Sabbath)
	.2	Liturgy
		Including *Siddurim* dealing specifically with Shabbat
	.21	Sephardic
	.22	Ashkenazic
	.23	Other Communities
	.24	Supplemental, Non-Traditional, and Modern

.25	Commentaries and Explanations
.3	Study and Teaching
.5	Literature
	See note under 236.5 *applying it to Shabbat*
.6	Program Material, Arts and Crafts, Music and Song; *Zemirot*
	Including *Oneg Shabbat*
.7	History and Development
.9	Special Shabbatot
.91	*Shuva* (Between Rosh Ha-Shanah and Yom Kippur)
.92	*Shekalim* (Precedes month of Adar)
.93	*Zakhor* (Precedes Purim)
.94	*Parah* (Precedes Shabbat ha-Hodesh)
.95	*Ha-Hodesh* (Precedes or falls on the first day of Nissan)
.96	*Ha-Gadol* (Precedes Pesah)
.97	*Shira* (Pesah)
.98	*Hazon* (Precedes the 9th of Av)
.99	*Nahamu* (Follows 9th of Av)
238	**High Holidays**
	Including the period beginning with *Selihot* and ending with Yom Kippur
.1	Laws, Customs, and Ceremonies
.11	Shofar
.2	Liturgy
	Mahzorim dealing specifically with the High Holy Day period including those for both Rosh Ha-Shanah and Yom Kippur
	Divide like 237.2
.29	*Selihot*
.3	Study and Teaching

	.5	Literature See note under 236.5 applying it to High Holidays
	.6	Program Material, Arts and Crafts, Music and Song
	.7	History and Development
239		**Rosh Ha-Shanah (New Year)** For liturgy, see 238.2
	.1	Laws, Customs, and Ceremonies
	.11	*Tashlikh* (Casting of Sins)
	.3	Study and Teaching
	.5	Literature See note under 236.5 applying it to Rosh Ha-Shanah
	.6	Program Material, Arts and Crafts, Music and Song
	.7	History and Development
240		**Yom Kippur (Day of Atonement)** For liturgy, see 238.2
	.1	Laws, Customs, and Ceremonies
	.11	*Kapparot* (Atonement)
	.3	Study and Teaching
	.5	Literature See note under 236.5 applying it to Yom Kippur
	.7	History and Development
241		***Shalosh Regalim* (Three Pilgrimage Festivals)**
	.2	Liturgy *Mahzorim* dealing specifically with the *Shalosh Regalim* Divide like 237.2. For individual holidays, see the specific holiday

242 Sukkot (Tabernacles)
- .1   Laws, Customs, and Ceremonies
- .11   Sukkah
- .12   *Arba'ah Minnim* (Four Species) including Lulav and Etrog
- .13   *Hoshanot* (Liturgical Poems)
- .2   Liturgy
         Divide like 237.2
- .3   Study and Teaching
- .5   Literature
         See note under 236.5 applying it to Sukkot
- .6   Program Material, Arts and Crafts, Music and Song
- .7   History and Development

243 Shemini Atzeret and Simhat Torah
- .1   Laws, Customs, and Ceremonies
- .2   Liturgy
         Divide like 237.2
- .3   Study and Teaching
- .5   Literature
         See note under 236.5 applying it to Shemini Atzeret and Simhat Torah
- .6   Program Material, Arts and Crafts, Music and Song
- .7   History and Development

244 Pesah (Passover)
- .1   Laws, Customs, and Ceremonies
- .11   *Bedikat Hametz* (Search for Leaven)
- .12   Seder
- .2   Liturgy
         Divide like 237.2

.29	*Haggadot*
.3	Study and Teaching
.5	Literature
	See note under 236.5 *applying it to Pesah*
.6	Program Material, Arts and Crafts, Music and Song
.7	History and Development
.9	*Sefirat Ha-Omer* (Counting of the Omer)

245 Shavuot (Pentecost)

.1	Laws, Customs, and Ceremonies
.2	Liturgy
	Divide like 237.2
.3	Study and Teaching
.5	Literature
	See note under 236.5 *applying it to Shavuot*
.6	Program Material, Arts and Crafts, Music and Song
.7	History and Development

246 Post-Biblical Festivals
Divide like 236

247 Hanukkah
Divide like 236

248 Tu Bi-Shevat (New Year for Trees)
Divide like 236

249 Purim
Divide like 236

.8	*Adloyada* (Purim Carnival)

| | .9 | Special Days of Purim
e.g., Shushan Purim |
|---|---|---|
| 250 | | Lag Ba-Omer
Divide like 236 |
| 251 | | Tu be-Av (15th of Av)
Divide like 236 |
| 253 | | Fast Days
Divide like 236. For Yom Kippur, see 240 |
| 254 | | Tzom Gedaliah (Fast of Gedaliah) |
| 255 | | Asarah B'Tevet (Tenth of Tevet) |
| 256 | | Ta'anit Esther (Fast of Esther) |
| 257 | | Shivah Asar B'Tammuz (Seventeenth of Tammuz) |
| 258 | | Tishah be-Av (Ninth of Av)
Divide like 236 |
| | .2 | *Liturgy* |
| | .21 | *Kinnot* |
| 259 | | Yom Ha-Atzma'ut (Israel Independence Day)
Divide like 236 |
| 260 | | Yom ha-Sho'ah u'Gevurah (Holocaust and Heroism Remembrance Day)
Divide like 236 |

261	Yom Ha-Zikkaron (Remembrance Day for Israeli soldiers) *Divide like 236*
262	Yom Yerushalayim *Divide like 236*
265	Rosh Hodesh (New Month)

270 Special Events and Occasions

271–282	Jewish Months
271	Nisan
272	Iyyar
273	Sivan
274	Tammuz
275	Av
276	Elul
277	Tishri
278	Heshvan
279	Kislev
280	Tevet

281	Shevat
282	Adar
	Including Adar Bet
285	Ecumenical Holidays and Observances
	e.g., Thanksgiving
286	Patriotic Holidays
	e.g., George Washington's Birthday
287	Universal Observances
	e.g., United Nations' Day

290 Comparative Religion

.1	Scriptures, Basic Religious Texts
.2	Central Personalities, Prophets
.3	Theology and Homiletics
.4	Organization and Governance
.5	Rituals and Symbols
.6	Internal Division, Sects
	Including Jews for Jesus
.7	History
.79	Biography
.8	Research and Criticism
.9	Study and Teaching
.91	Dictionaries and Encyclopedias

291 Paganism

Divide like **290**. For Ancient Near Eastern religions, see **092**

292	Christianity
	Divide like 290
.1	Christian Scriptures
.69	Mormonism

293	Islam
	Divide like 290
.1	Koran

294	Oriental Religions
.1	Buddhism
.2	Hinduism
.3	Confucianism

295	Zoroastrianism

296	Other Religions

300–399

Jewish Education

300 **Jewish Education**
   .3   Addresses, Essays, and Lectures
   .5   Anthologies
   .6   Associations, Directories, and Societies
   .9   Yearbooks and Special Events Publications

301   Philosophy of Jewish Education

304   Dictionaries and Encyclopedias

305   General Education
   .1   Philosophy
   .3   Addresses, Essays, and Lectures
   .4   Dictionaries and Encyclopedias
   .5   Anthologies
   .6   Associations, Directories, and Societies
   .7   History
   .9   Yearbooks and Special Events Publications

307   History of Jewish Education
For Jewish education in Israel, see 308; Jewish education in U.S., see 310, other countries, divide like 740–797.

308   Jewish Education in Israel
Divide like 305. For material on Israeli education in general, see 872.

310   Jewish Education in the United States
- .3   Addresses, Essays, and Lectures
- .4   Dictionaries and Encyclopedias
- .5   Anthologies
- .6   Associations, Directories, and Societies
       e.g., Jewish Education Service of North America (JESNA)
- .9   Yearbooks and Special Events Publications

311   Philosophy of Jewish Education in U.S.

312   History of Jewish Education in U.S.

313   Systems and Forms
- .1   Day Schools
- .2   Afternoon Hebrew Schools
- .21   Community Schools
- .22   Synagogue Schools
- .3   Sunday Schools
- .4   Secular Schools
- .41   Yiddish Schools
- .5   Yeshivot

315 School Administration
- .5 Early Childhood Education
  Including Nursery and Kindergarten
- .6 Elementary
- .7 Junior High
- .8 High School

316 Central Administrative Agencies
Including Bureaus

317 Budgeting and Finance

318 School Facility Planning, Architecture, Construction, and Maintenance

319 Transportation

320 School Equipment
For audiovisual, see **328.1**

321 Community Relations
- .1 School-Federation Relationships
- .2 School-Synagogue Relations
- .3 School-Home Relationships
  Including PTA
- .4 Interschool Relations

325 Teaching
Including material describing teaching as a profession
For methodology of teaching specific subjects, see **340–363**

326 Teacher Training
        Including methods of teaching

327 Classroom Organization and Discipline

328 Teaching Aids
  .1   Audiovisual

329 Testing

330 *Curriculum*
        Including general works dealing with curricula

331 Curricula for the Jewish School
  .5   Integrated Curriculum
        Use for curricula designed to incorporate both Judaic and general studies

332 Early Childhood Education
  .1   Nursery and Kindergarten

333 Elementary Education

334 Secondary Education

335 Day Schools
  .1   Traditional Yeshivot
  .2   Modern Orthodox
  .3   Conservative
  .4   Reform and Liberal
  .5   Secular
  .6   Yiddish

336	**Afternoon Hebrew School**
.1	Elementary
.2	Secondary

337	**Afternoon Secular Schools**
	Divide like 336

338	**Afternoon Yiddish Schools**
	Divide like 336

339	**Special Classes**
.1	Art
.2	Drama
.3	Music

*In a Teachers' Reference Center, topic areas may also be designated by using a "T" prefix with the same numbers as those used in the general collection

340	***Early Childhood Education—Methodology and Materials***
.3	Textbooks and workbooks

341	**Nursery**

342	**Kindergarten**

345	***Elementary and Intermediate Education—Methodology and Materials***
	Divide like 340

346   Bible
                Divide like 340
    .5   Dramatics

347   Religion, Liturgy, Customs, and Ceremonies
                Divide like 340

348   Language
                Divide like 340
    .1   Reading
    .2   Writing

349   History and Current Events
                Divide like 340

350   Special Topics
    .1   Keren Ami

351   Extracurricular Activities
    .1   Assembly
    .2   Junior Congregations
    .3   Arts and Crafts
    .4   Music
    .5   Dramatics and Reader's Theater
    .6   Story-telling

355   Secondary Education
                Divide like 340

356   Bible
                Divide like 340

| 357 | Halakhah, Customs, and Ceremonies
Divide like 340 |
|---|---|
| 358 | Aggadah
Divide like 340 |
| 359 | Language and Grammar
Divide like 340 |
| 360 | Literature and Arts
Divide like 340 |
| 361 | Jewish Life and History
Divide like 340 |
| 362 | Israel and Zionism
Divide like 340 |
| 363 | Extracurricular Activities
Divide like 340 |

365 *Higher Education*

For study and teaching of specific subjects see the classification of the subject, i.e., 012.3 study and teaching of Bible

366	Curriculum
367	Administration
368	Student Activities

369		College Publications
	.1	Bulletins
	.2	Yearbooks

375 Adult and Continuing Education
Including Jewish Chautauqua Society

376	Family Education
380	Educational Group Work

381		Summer Camps
	.1	Day Camps
	.2	Hebrew-Speaking Camps
	.3	Zionist Camps
	.4	Directories

382 Youth Movements
Technical materials relating to the organization and functioning of youth movements
For histories, see **641**; *for program materials, see specific topics, e.g., Oneg Shabbat* **237.6**

385 Special Education

386 Education of the Physically Handicapped
Including blind (Braille), deaf, etc.

387 Education for the Mentally Handicapped

388 Education for the Learning Disabled

389	Games and Activities

> *For games designed specifically as teaching aids for particular subjects, see respective subject, e.g., Elementary Hebrew, 348*

390 Psychology

391	Educational Psychology
392	Learning Theory
393	Psychological Testing
394	Psychological and Therapeutic Counseling
395	Personality Theory
396	Group Psychology
397	Child Psychology
.2	Child Development
.21	Infant and Preschool
.22	Elementary
.23	Adolescence
.5	Child Abuse

> Effects of mental, physical, and sexual abuse on children

398	Self-Help
399	Psychiatry and Psychoanalysis

400–499

Hebrew, Jewish Languages, and Sciences

400 ***Hebrew Language***
　　　Including history of Hebrew language
　　　For Biblical Hebrew, see **004**; *for Mishnaic Hebrew, see* **102.4**
　.5　　Renaissance of Spoken Hebrew
　.6　　Academy of Hebrew Language

401　Orthography (Spelling) and Alphabets
　.5　　Vocalization
　.6　　Abbreviations

402　Etymology, Derivation, Semantics

403　Dictionaries (Hebrew/Hebrew Dictionaries)
　.1　　Combined (Hebrew-English, English-Hebrew)
　.2　　Hebrew-English
　.3　　English-Hebrew

.4	Hebrew-Other
.5	Other-Hebrew
.9	Glossaries
404	Idiomatic Dictionaries
405	Synonyms, Homonyms
406	Phonology, Phonetics
.1	Pronunciation
	e.g., material on Ashkenazic and Sephardic pronunciation
.2	Accent and Intonation
407	Prosody
408	Hebrew Grammar
.1	Syntax
.2	Nouns
.3	Adjectives, Articles
.4	Pronouns
.5	Verbs
.6	Particles
409	Textbooks
	Including conversation manuals

415 *Aramaic*

416	Etymology, Derivations, Semantics
417	Orthography, Alphabets
	Divide like 403

418	Study and Teaching
419	Dictionaries
.5	Idiomatic
420	Synonyms and Homonyms
421	Phonology, Phonetics, Pronunciation
422	Prosody
423	Grammar
424	Self-Study Texts

425 *Ladino (Judezimo)*
Including various forms of Judeo-Spanish

426	Etymology, Derivations, Semantics
427	Orthography, Alphabets
	Divide like 403
428	Study and Teaching
429	Dictionaries
.5	Idiomatic
430	Synonyms and Homonyms
431	Phonology, Phonetics, Pronunciation

432	Prosody
433	Grammar
434	Textbooks

435 Yiddish

436	Etymology, Derivation, Semantics
437	Orthography, Alphabets
	Divide like 403
438	Study and Teaching
439	Dictionaries
.5	Idiomatic
440	Synonyms and Homonyms
441	Phonology, Phonetics, Pronunciation
442	Prosody
443	Grammar
444	Textbooks

445 Other Jewish Languages

446	Judeo-Persian
.1	Etymology, Derivatives, Semantics
.2	Orthography and Alphabets

.3 Study and Teaching
.4 Dictionaries
.5 Synonyms, Homonyms
.6 Phonology, Phonetics, Pronunciation
.7 Prosody
.8 Grammar

447 Judeo-Arabic
Divide like 446

448 Judeo-Greek
Divide like 446

449 Judeo-Italian
Divide like 446

455 *Semitic and Ancient Near Eastern Languages*
Divide like 446

456 Akkadian
Divide like 446

457 Phoenician
Divide like 446

458 Moabite
Divide like 446

459 Ugaritic
Divide like 446

460   Amorite
            Divide like 446

461   Arabic
            Divide like 446

462   Ethiopic
            Divide like 446

463   Other

470   Comparative Linguistics
   .1   Descriptive
   .2   Historical
   .3   Geographical
   .5   Language and Culture

471   Semantics

480   Sciences
            Including material on Jews and the sciences, Jewish contributions to the sciences, and Jewish scientific concerns and endeavors
   .6   Classical Jewish Science Translations
            Translations by Jews of classical scientific material particularly in the medieval period
   .7   History of Science
   .798   Collective Biographies of Jewish Scientists
   .799   Individual Biographies of Jewish Scientists

481   Mathematics
            Divide like 480

482	**Astronomy**
Divide like 480
483	**Physics**
Divide like 480
484	**Chemistry**
Divide like 480
485	**Geology**
Divide like 480
486	**Biology**
Divide like 480
487	**Botany**
Divide like 480
488	**Zoology**
Divide like 480
489	**Engineering and Electronics**
Divide like 480
.8	Computer Science and Programs
490	**Medicine**
Divide like 480. For medicine in the Bible, see 012.1; for specific health issues, see 656
.5	Medical Ethics

500–599

Jewish Literature

500 Jewish Literature—History and Development

Works on Jewish literature by form
For works on the history and development of Jewish literature by region and language, use 501–523. For the literary work of individual authors, use 560–567; for anthologies, use 550–558; for criticism and analysis, use 530–537.

- .1 Poetry
- .2 Drama
- .3 Fiction, Short Stories
- .4 Literary Essays
- .5 Oratory
- .6 Letters, Ethical Wills
- .7 Humor, Satire, Wit
- .9 Special Topics

501-503
Covers cultural areas that had distinct geographic identities prior to the period 1939-1948. Material covering the same areas subsequent to that period should be classified in 504-525 as appropriate

501 Sephardic Literature—History and Development
Principally Spain, Portugal, Italy, Greece, Turkey and the Ottoman Empire, and the Levant. Works on the history of the literature of the Sephardic culture area including Ladino regardless of geographical boundaries
Divide like 500

502 Literature of Oriental Jewry—History and Development
Principally Persia, Babylonia, Yemen, and other Jewries of the Arabic countries. Including Judeo-Arabic and Judeo-Persian
Divide like 500

503 Ashkenazic Literature—History and Development
Principally Germany, Northern France, and Central and Eastern Europe. Works on the literature of the Ashkenazic culture area including Yiddish regardless of geographical boundaries
For works about the literature of Ashkenazic Jews whose writings are not uniquely Ashkenazic, or Yiddish, see geographical locations
Divide like 500

504	European Jewish Literature Since World War II—History and Development *For works on the literature of the Jews of Great Britain, see 522* *Divide like 500*
510	Hebrew Literature—History and Development Including works on Hebrew literature during the modern period regardless of geographical boundaries. Works dealing with the literature in Hebrew written before the modern revival of Hebrew literature (the mid-eighteenth century) should be classified by culture area *Divide like 500*
.8	*Haskalah* (1781–1881)
.9	Zionist Renaissance
511	Israeli Literature—History and Development *Divide like 500*
520	U.S. Jewish Literature—History and Development *Divide like 500*
521	Canadian Jewish Literature—History and Development *Divide like 500*
522	British Jewish Literature—History and Development *Divide like 500*

523   Other Jewish Literature in the English Language—History and Development
        Including South Africa, Australia, New Zealand, etc.
        Divide like 500

530   *Jewish Literature—Criticism and Analysis*

   .736   Holocaust

531   Poetry

532   Drama

533   Fiction, Short Stories

534   Literary Essays

535   Oratory

536   Letters, Ethical Wills

537   Humor, Satire, Wit

540   *Jewish Literature—Study and Teaching*

541   Jewish Literature—Dictionaries and Encyclopedias

542	Literary Societies—Transactions, Reports, Publications
543	Jewish Literature—Addresses, Essays, Lectures

550 Jewish Literature—Anthologies and Selections
Divide like 500
.8   Quotations

551	Anthologies—Sephardic Literature *See note under 501; divide like 500*
552	Anthologies—Oriental Jewish Literature *See note under 502; divide like 500*
553	Anthologies—Ashkenazic Literature *See note under 503; divide like 500*
554	Anthologies—European Jewish Literature *See note under 504; divide like 500*
555	Anthologies—Hebrew Literature *See note under 510; divide like 500*
556	Anthologies—Israeli Literature *Divide like 500*

557   Anthologies—English Language Jewish Literature
>Includes literature written originally in the English language; for translations, use the section where the original would be classified (e.g., an anthology of translated Israeli Hebrew literature, 556)
>*Divide like 500*

558   Anthologies—Latin American Jewish Literature
>*Divide like 500*

560   *Jewish Literature—Individual Works*

>Use 560 for collected works by a single author. Use 561–567 for genre and arrange by author within respective form of literature

.799   Biography of individual authors

561   Poetry
.736   Holocaust Poetry

562   Drama

563   Short Stories
>Individual works of fiction should be classified in a separate section arranged alphabetically by author

564   Literary Essays

565	Oratory
566	Letters, Ethical Wills
567	Humor, Satire, Wit
580	Literary Periodicals, Magazines, Reviews Including anthologies of selections from periodicals
590	***General Literature Related to Jews and Judaism*** Includes literature written by non-Jews about Jews and Judaism. Use also for general literature that has been translated into Hebrew *Divide like 500*
591	Classical Literature Greek, Latin
592	Arabic Literature
593	Germanic Literature
594	Hispanic Literature Spanish, Portuguese, Catalan, Latin America
595	Slavic Literatures Russian, Polish, etc.
596	Romance Literature French, Italian, etc.

597 English Literature

598 North American Literature
Including Canada

599 Other Literatures

600–699

The Jewish Community: Society and the Arts

600   Jewish Social Institutions and Behavior
Those aspects of Jewish life pertaining to the structure and functioning of the Jewish people and their individual behavior within the framework of Jewish society. Excludes biblical period and life, and modern Israel
.2   Addresses, Essays, Lectures
.3   Study and Teaching
.4   Dictionaries and Encyclopedias
.6   Research and Criticism

601   Social History
Historical studies of Jewish social institutions and behavior. The numbers .1–.9 reflect the major divisions in Jewish social history, di-

vided historically by period where applicable. The historical periods are further divided on the basis of the regional alignment of the Jewish communities. For recorded events within specific historical periods, see the 700s.

- .1 *Keneset Ha-Gedolah* and Tannaitic Periods (5th Century BCE–3rd Century CE)
- .2 Gaonic, Middle, and High Talmudic Oriental (4th–17th Centuries)
- .3 Early, Middle, and High Talmudic Mediterranean (4th–17th Centuries)
- .4 Early, Middle, and High Talmudic North European (4th–17th Centuries)
- .5 Late Talmudic Western European (17th–19th Centuries)
- .6 Late Talmudic Eastern European (17th–19th Centuries)
- .7 Late Talmudic Near Eastern (17th–19th Centuries)
- .8 Modern Non-Western (20th Century–)
- .9 Modern Western (20th Century–)

602   Biological Characteristics of Jewish Populations
Including material on genetic pattern, blood groups, anatomical form, etc.

603   Ethnography
Including material that deals with special cultures or groups

604   Migrations
- .3 Immigration Laws and Policies
- .5 Refugee Studies

605	Social Statistics
606	Demography, Population Studies; Vital Statistics Includes community surveys and census reports Divide like 740-794
607	Social Classes, Reference Groups
608	Social Psychology

610 Personal and Social Customs
Customs associated with specific regions, localities, or time periods that are not explicitly embodied in *halakhah* (religious law) or universally accepted within Jewish tradition
Divide like 601

611	Birth and Sex Customs Divide like 601. For halakhic aspect see 222.1 and 222.4
612	Personal Health and Hygiene Including treatment of illness, medical theories, customs of cleanliness, etc. Divide like 601
613	Treatment of the Dead, Mourning Including bereavement and coping Divide like 601. For halakhic aspect, see 222.5

614		**Home Customs** *Divide like 601*
615		**Foods** *Divide like 601. For cooking and culinary art, see 699. For Kashrut, see 221.1*
616		**Etiquette** Canons of socially acceptable personal behavior *Divide like 601*
617		**Costume** *Divide like 601*
618		**Public and Social Customs** Canons of acceptable group behavior *Divide like 601*
619		**Women's Position and Treatment**
	.2	Customs and Ceremonies
	.6	Feminism
	.7	History
	.9	Special Topics

620 *Jewish Political Structure and Governance*

Including materials on Jewish national and communal self-government (excluding biblical and modern Israel), democracy in the Jewish community, and modern quasi-governmental organizations, such as Jewish federations and community councils
Divide like 601

621 Theories of Governmental and Communal Organization and Operations
> Theories of Jewish self-government, discussions of the organic Jewish community, the *Kehillah*, etc.
> For abstract political thought, see **136.42**

622 National and Multi-community Structures and Governments
> Including Palestinian Patriarchate, Council of Four Lands, Board of Deputies of British Jews, Canadian Jewish Congress, Council of Jewish Federations
> *Divide like* **601**

623 Local Governments and Community Organization
> Including *Kehillot*, Jewish Federations, Jewish Community councils
> *Divide like* **601**

624 Councils, Governing Assemblies
> The organization and operation of councilar law-making and law-interpreting bodies— e.g., *Keneset ha-Gedolah*, the Gerusia
> *Divide like* **601**

.1   Sanhedrin

625 Courts, Judicial Institutions
> e.g., *Bet Din*, Tribunals
> *Divide like* **601**

626   **The Executive Function, Heads of Governing Bodies**
> Including kingship under the Hasmoneans, the Exilarch, the Naggid, Nasi, Presidents, and Executive Heads
> *Divide like* 601

627   **Fiscal Institution, Taxation, and Fundraising**
> Raising funds for Jewish national and communal purposes, e.g., *Keren Hayesod*, United Jewish Appeal
> *Divide like* 601

628   **Community Administrative Organization**
> Includes any Jewish body, institution, or organization and any discussion of its internal administration
> *Divide like* 601

629   **Political Participation**
> Membership or citizenship, suffrage, representation, elections
> *Divide like* 601

630   **Status, Rights, and Obligations of the Individual**
> Including individual freedoms and censorship

634   **External Affairs**
> The relations between organized Jewish communities and the external world, e.g., the Jewish community and the Vatican
> *Divide like* 601

635   Communal Institutions and Organizations
Divide like 601

636   The Synagogue and Religious Organizations
Includes Congregations and *Havurot*
For religious rites, see 224; for architecture, see 672

.1   Structure and Organization
.2   The Synagogue Rabbinate; Cantorate
    e.g., Rabbinical Assembly of America
.3   Subsidiary Bodies
    e.g., Brotherhoods, Sisterhoods, *Hevrot*, etc.
.7   History
.8   Organizations of Synagogues
    e.g., United Synagogue of America, Union of Progressive Synagogues, Young Israel
    Divide like 740–794

637   "Representative" and Political Purpose Organizations
Including "defense" organizations, e.g., Anti-Defamation League
Divide like 740–794

638   Health and Welfare Institutions
.1   Hospitals
.2   Aid to Handicapped
.3   Services for the Aged
.4   Children and Youth Services
.5   Social Services
    e.g., HIAS, Joint Distribution Committee (JDC)

.6 Economic Assistance
e.g., free loan societies
.7 Burial Services
e.g., *Hevra Kaddisha*
.8 Services to the Military
Including chaplains

639 Service Organizations
e.g., *B'nai Brith*, National Council for Jewish Women
Divide like 740–794
.3 *Landsmannschaften*

640 Educational Institutions and Organizations
.1 Rabbinical Seminaries, *Yeshivot*
.2 Teachers' Colleges
.3 Libraries and Archives
.4 Jewish Institutions of Higher Learning
Including colleges and universities under Jewish auspices; e.g., Hebrew Union College, Jewish Theological Seminary, Yeshiva University
.5 Continuing Education Institutes
e.g., CLAL Hartman Institute
.7 Research Institutes
e.g., YIVO
.8 Policy Studies Institutes
e.g., Jerusalem Center for Public Affairs

641 Youth Organizations
Divide like 740–794. For Zionist parties, see 810, Zionist youth organizations, e.g., Habonim 812.7

| 642 | Cultural Institutions and Organizations
e.g., *Histadrut Ivrit*, National Jewish Welfare Board
Divide like 740–974 |

| 643 | Social Organizations
Divide like 740–794 |

| 644 | International Organizations and Institutions
e.g., Alliance Israelite Universelle, ORT
Divide like 601 |

645 Jewish Economic Institutions and Behavior
Divide like 740–794

| 646 | Economic Conditions
Divide like 740–794 |

| 647 | Economic Activities, Occupations
Including related professional organizations |
| .1 | Agriculture
e.g., Jewish Agricultural Society |
| .2 | Artisans and Craftsmen |
| .3 | Trade and Finance, Banking, Merchants, Commerce
Including moneylending |
.4	Law
.5	Medicine and Pharmacy
.6	Science and Technology
.7	Social Service

.8 Education
.9 Other

648 Labor, Conditions of Work
Divide like 740–794
.1 Jewish Guilds
.2 Jewish Labor Unions
.3 Jewish Labor Movements
e.g., The Jewish Workers Bund, Workmen's Circle, Jewish Labor Committee
For labor movements in Israel, see 863

650 Social Conditions and Problems

Including moral conditions, intermarriage, divorce, juvenile delinquency, housing, recreations, standard of living, etc.
Divide like 740–794. For Jewish responses to general social conditions and problems, see 667; for Israel, see 869

651 Sexual Behavior
.5 Abortion
.7 Homosexuality

652 Marriage and Family
.1 Divorce
.2 Intermarriage and Interdating
.3 Birth Control
.4 Adoption and infertility
.5 Adultery
.6 Widowhood

.7	Issues in Parenting
	e.g., single parents, working parents
.9	Polygamy

653	Aging, Geriatrics

654	Crime and Juvenile Delinquency

655	Jewish Identity
	Including non-halakhic works on who is a Jew
.5	Assimilation

656	Health and Illness
.1	Mental Health
.3	Euthanasia
.5	Alcoholism
.6	Suicide

657	Settlement Patterns, Housing

658	Social Relations
.5	Poverty
	Including homelessness

659	Environmental Problems, Ecology, Conservation

660 *The Jews in the World Order*

Position of Jews within or in relation to major or "host" civilization

.1 Ancient Near East, Persian Civilization

.2 Hellenistic World, Hellenism
   For Hellenistic thought, see 165
.3 Roman Empire
.4 Islamic World
.5 Medieval Christian Europe
.6 Renaissance and Reformation Europe
.7 Modern Europe
.8 American Civilization
.9 Contemporary (20th Century–)

661 General Relations Between Jews and Non-Jews
.3 Christian-Jewish Relations
   Including the Catholic Church
.5 Arab and Muslim-Jewish Relations
   For Israel-Arab relations, see 890.5
.7 Black-Jewish Relations
.9 Apostasy, Proselytizing of Jews
.91 Cults
   Including Christian missionaries

662 Anti-Semitism
   Including influential cases, e.g., Damascus Affair, Mortara Case, Dreyfus Affair
   Divide like 740–794
.95 Christian Apologetics
.96 Neo-Nazism

665 Jewish Influences on World Civilization
   e.g., education, social welfare, economic systems, etc.

666	The Influence of Individual Jews
667	Jewish Responses to Social Conditions and Problems

        Including the Jewish attitudes toward poverty, warfare, human rights

668	Jewish Political Behavior

        In the context of general political situations
        For the political behavior of Jews within their own political systems, see 629

670 *Jewish Graphic and Plastic Arts*

        Including comprehensive works of Jewish artists

.1	Addresses, Essays, Lectures
.2	Philosophy
.3	Study and Teaching
.4	Dictionaries and Encyclopedias
.5	Directories
.6	Societies
.7	History
.8	Compendia, Outlines
.9	Catalogs

671	Architecture
.2	Theories
.6	Societies
.7	History

672	Synagogue Architecture

        Divide like 740–794

673		**Civic Architecture**
	.1	Schools
	.2	Community Centers
	.3	Hospitals
	.4	Homes for the Aged
	.5	Cemeteries
	.6	*Mikvaot* (Ritual Baths)
		For halakhic aspect, see **221.5**
	.7	Other Community Buildings

674   **Jewish Ceremonial Art**

675		**Plastic Arts, Sculpture**
	.1	Gems, Cameos, etc.
	.2	Seal, Stamps, Signets
	.3	Carving of Horn, Bone, etc.
		Including preparation of a shofar from an artistic point of view
	.4	Woodcarving
	.5	Stone Carving

676   **Numismatics: Coins, Metals**
           Artistic and historic only

677		**Ceramic Arts**
	.1	Pottery
	.2	Mosaics

678   **Metal Arts, Jewelry**

679		**Arts and Crafts**
	.1	Woodworking
	.2	Textile Arts, Leather working

.3	Puppetry
.4	Paper
	Including papercuts and origami
.5	Plastics, Synthetics
.6	Basketmaking
.7	Ornamental Leather
.8	Decals
.9	Glasswork
680	**Fancy Work, Art, Needlework**
.1	Laces
.2	Tapestry
.3	Needlework
.5	Batik
.6	Handmade rugs
.7	Waxwork
681	**Drawing and Painting**
.5	Calligraphy
682	**Engraving**
.9	Postage Stamps
683	**Photography**

685 *Jewish Music*
Divide like 670

686	**Sacred Music**
.1	Cantillation
.2	*Hazanut* (Cantorial music)
	For liturgy, see 230

.3 Choir Music
.4 Hymns
.5 Cantatas
.6 Oratorios

687   Vocal Music
Including folk songs
.1 Collections of Songs
.11 Children's Songs
.2 Hebrew
Including Israeli songs
.3 Ladino
.4 Yiddish
.5 Jewish Songs in Other Languages

688   Dramatic Music
.1 Operas
.2 Cantatas
.3 Musical Productions

689   Instrumental Music

690   Public Entertainment, Mass Media
Divide like 670

691   Dramatic Arts, Theater
Divide like 740–794; for Israel, see 883
.1 Plays
Plays on individual holidays may be classified in .6 of the specific holiday
.2 Public Fetes, Pageants, Festivals

692	Motion Pictures
693	Radio and Television
694	Concerts
695	Dance
.1	Ballet
.2	Interpretive Dance
.3	Folk Dancing
696	Public Games and Sports
.6	Maccabiah Societies
.9	Indoor Games
697	Other Amusements

699 Cooking and Culinary Arts
Including cookbooks

.1	Holidays
.11	Pesach
.2	Regional
	e.g., Ashkenazic, Sephardic, Oriental
.25	Ethnic (non-Jewish) Kosher
	e.g., Chinese, Italian
.3	Vegetarian and Health Oriented
.4	Children
.9	Special (Jewish)
	Including specialty cookbooks for soups, challah, cholent, etc.

700–799

Jewish History, Geography, Biography

700 **Jewish History**
For the history of the Jewish religion, see 207; material directly related to the Bible, see 001–099. For explanation of historical periodization, see the Introduction. Because all periodization is approximate, classification should be on the basis of the major concern of the book being classified

701 **Addresses, Essays, and Lectures**
Including historical Festschriften; for general Festschriften, see 910

702 **Philosophy, Theories of History**

703 **Study and Teaching**

704 **Dictionaries, Encyclopedias**

705   Chronologies, Charts, Outlines

706   Societies, Transactions, Reports
           e.g., Jewish Historical Society of England

707   Historiography

708   Atlases, Maps

709   Special Topics
           i.e., military history, etc.

710   The Emergence of the Jewish People (20th–5th Centuries BCE)
           Including materials written explicitly as histories of the period. For biblical history, see 007

711   Patriarchal Period (20th–14th Centuries BCE)

712   The Egyptian Exile

713   The Exodus (14th–13th Centuries BCE)

715   The First Commonwealth

716   The Tribal Confederacy (13th–11th Centuries BCE)
    .1   The Conquest of Canaan
    .2   Period of the Judges
    .3   The Reign of Saul (1029–1005 BCE)

717	The Davidic Monarchy (1000–586 BCE)
.1	The United Monarchy (1004–928 BCE)
.2	The Kingdom of Judah (928–586 BCE)

| 718 | The Kingdom of Israel |

| 719 | The Babylonian Exile |

720 The Emergence of Talmudic Judaism (5th Century BCE–8th Century CE)
Including overall treatments of the Jews in the Greco-Roman period

| 721 | The Second Commonwealth (538 BCE–135 CE) |

722	*Knesset ha-Gedolah* and Its Successors (440–165 BCE)
.1	The Restoration
.2	The Jews Under Persian Hegemony
.3	The Jews Under Hellenistic Hegemony
	For Hellenism, see 660.2

| 724 | *Galut* (Jews in exile and in diaspora) |
| | Including general or overall treatments of Jewish exile and dispersion |

725	Tannaitic Period (165 BCE–200 CE)
.1	Pharisees
.2	Sadducees
.3	Essenes

726 The Hasmoneans (165–66 BCE)
  .1   The Maccabean Revolt
  .2   The Hasmonean Kings

727 The Jews Under the Roman Empire (66 BCE–66 CE)
  .3   The Jewish Roman War and Its Aftermath (66 BCE–132 CE)
  .5   The Bar Cochba Revolt and Its Aftermath (132–200)

728 Amoraitic Period (c. 200–500)

729 Gaonic (Early Talmudic) Period (c. 500–800)

730 *The Era of Normative Judaism (9th–19th Centuries)*
Including overall treatment of the Jews in the Middle Ages

731 Middle Talmudic Period (c. 800–1200)

732 High Talmudic Period (c. 1200–1600)

733 Late Talmudic Period (c. 1600–1900)

734 Emancipation and Enlightenment
  .3   The *Haskalah* (1770–1880)

735 The Contemporary Era (20th Century–)
.1   World War I
.2   Between the World Wars
.3   World War II

736 The Nazi Holocaust (1933–1945)
For Israel, see 827.8; for Yom ha-sho'ah (Holocaust Remembrance Day), see 260

.01   Nazism and Related Anti-Semitic Movements
      Including biographies of Nazis
.02   Genocide
.08   Maps and Atlases
.1   Concentration Camps
.2   Resistance
.3   War Crimes, Punishments
      Including Eichmann Trial
.4   Refugees and Rescue
.41   Righteous Gentiles
.5   Personal Narratives
.6   Memorials and Organizations
.8   Reparations and Restitution
.9   Special Topics
.91   Holocaust Revisionism
.92   Survivors
.93   Second Generation

737 Post World War II

740 The Jews of the Middle East
Excluding the Mediterranean countries. For general and political works on countries in the Middle East, use 891–899

.1 Late Monarchic
.2 *Knesset ha-Gedolah* and Its Successors (440–165 BCE)
.3 Tannaitic (165 BCE–200 CE)
.4 Amoraitic (c. 200–500)
.5 Gaonic (c. 500–800)
.6 Middle Talmudic (c. 800–1200)
.7 High Talmudic (c. 1600–1900)
.9 Modern (1900–)

741 Babylonia (Iraq)
Divide like 740

742 Persia (Iran) and Afghanistan
Divide like 740

743 Bokhara and Turkestan
Divide like 740

744 Arabian Peninsula and Yemen
Divide like 740

750 *Sephardic and Mediterranean Jewry*

751 Egypt
Divide like 740

752 North Africa
Including materials on North African Jewry in general and works dealing specifically with Libya, Tunisia, and Algeria
Divide like 740. For works dealing specifically with Morocco, see 753

753 Morocco
>Divide like 740

754 Syria and Lebanon
>Divide like 740

755 Iberian Peninsula, Spain
>Including Moorish and Christian Spain and the various Iberian kingdoms
>For Inquisition, see 758.9
- .1 165 BCE–800 CE
- .2 800–1200
- .3 1200–1600
- .4 1600–1900
- .5 1900–
- .6 Castile
- .7 Aragon
- .8 Portugal

756 Italian Peninsula, Italy
>Divide like 740

757 Balkans and Asia Minor
- .2 Byzantine Empire
- .5 Ottoman Empire and Turkey
- .6 Greece
- .7 Yugoslavia
>Including successor states
- .71 Serbia
- .72 Croatia
- .73 Bosnia
- .74 Slovenia

.8 Bulgaria
.9 Albania

758 The Marranos
.9 The Inquisition

759 Sephardic Dispersion
For material prior to World War I. After World War I, see individual country

760 *Ashkenazic and Eastern European Jewry*
Divide like 740

761 Germany
.1 165 BCE–800 CE
.2 800–1200
.3 1200–1600
.4 1600–1900
.5 1900–1945
.6 1945–
.7 Prussia
Includes Jews in post World War II Germany

762 Central Europe
.1 Hungary
.2 Switzerland
.3 Czech Republic (including former Czechoslovakia)
.35 Slovakia
.4 Austria

763	Eastern Europe	
.4	Latvia	
.5	Estonia	
.6	Poland	
.7	Lithuania	
.8	Rumania	

764	Russia (Including the former Soviet Union)	
.2	Central Asian Republics	
.3	Belarus	
.5	Armenia	
.6	Ukraine	
.7	Moldavia (Including former Bessarabia)	

765 Western European Jewry
Divide like 740

766	Great Britain	
	Divide like 761.1–.5	
.6	Scotland	
.7	Ireland	

767	France	
	Divide like 761-1–.5	
.9	Provence	

768	Low Countries	
.1	Netherlands	
.2	Belgium	
.3	Luxembourg	

769		**Scandinavian Countries**
	.1	Sweden
	.2	Norway
	.3	Denmark
	.4	Finland
	.5	Iceland

770 *United States Jewry*
- .1 Addresses, Essays, and Lectures
- .2 Philosophy, Theories of History
- .3 Study and Teaching
- .4 Dictionaries, Encyclopedias
- .5 Chronologies, Charts, Outlines
- .6 Societies, Transactions, Reports
- .7 Historiography
- .8 Atlases, Maps
- .9 Special Topics

771 Jewish Settlement in the United States (1621–1920)
- .1 "Sephardic" Immigration (1621–1815)
- .2 Revolutionary War
- .3 "German" Immigration (1815–1880)
- .4 Civil War
- .5 "Eastern European" Immigration (1880–1920)
- .6 World War I

772 The Established Jewish Community (1918–)
- .1 Interwar Period (1918–1948)
- .2 World War II
- .3 Postwar Period (1948–)

700–799

773 New England States
- .1 Maine
- .2 New Hampshire
- .3 Vermont
- .4 Massachusetts
- .5 Rhode Island
- .6 Connecticut

774 Middle Eastern States
- .1 New York
- .11 New York City
- .12 Lower East Side
- .2 New Jersey
- .3 Pennsylvania
- .4 Delaware
- .5 Maryland
- .6 District of Columbia

775 Near Western States
  Including Middle West
- .1 Ohio
- .2 Indiana
- .3 Illinois
- .4 Michigan
- .5 Wisconsin

776 Northwestern States
  Including West
- .1 Minnesota
- .2 South Dakota
- .3 North Dakota
- .4 Montana
- .5 Iowa

    .6   Nebraska
    .7   Kansas
    .8   Colorado
    .9   Wyoming

777   Far Western States
    .1   California
    .2   Nevada
    .3   Utah
    .4   Washington
    .5   Oregon
    .6   Idaho
    .7   Alaska
    .8   Hawaii

778   Southwestern States
    .1   Missouri
    .2   Arkansas
    .3   Texas
    .4   Oklahoma
    .5   New Mexico
    .6   Arizona

779   Southern States: Upper South
    .1   Virginia
    .2   West Virginia
    .3   Kentucky
    .4   North Carolina
    .5   Tennessee

780   Southern States: Deep South
    .1   South Carolina
    .2   Georgia

.3 Florida
.4 Alabama
.5 Mississippi
.6 Louisiana

781 U.S. Territories
.1 Puerto Rico
.2 Virgin Islands

784 *Canadian Jewry*
.1 Maritime Provinces
.2 Quebec
.3 Ontario
.4 Manitoba
.5 Saskatchewan
.6 Alberta
.7 British Columbia

785 *South American Jewry*
.1 Argentina
.2 Bolivia
.3 Brazil
.4 Chile
.5 Columbia
.6 Ecuador
.7 Paraguay
.8 Peru
.9 Uruguay

786 *Caribbean Jewry*
.1 Venezuela
.2 Guiana

- .3 Cuba
- .4 West Indies
    Including Jamaica
- .5 Dutch West Indies and Surinam

787 Mexico and Central American Jewry
- .1 Mexico
- .2 Guatemala
- .3 Honduras
- .4 Nicaragua
- .5 El Salvador
- .6 Costa Rica
- .7 Panama

790 African Jewry
- .1 Ethiopia
    For Operations Solomon and Moses, see 868
- .2 South Africa
- .3 Zimbabwe (formerly Rhodesia)
- .4 Kenya
- .5 Congo
- .6 Former French Africa
- .7 Former British Africa

792 Asian Jewry
For Jews of the Middle East, see 740; for Jews of the former Soviet Union, see 764.5
- .1 India and Pakistan
- .2 China
    Including Hong Kong
- .3 Japan

.4	Burma
.5	Singapore

794 Oceania
.1	Australia
.2	New Zealand
.3	Philippines

795 Geography
Excluding maps and atlases

796 Travel Guides
Use for general travel guides; for specific countries and states, divide like 740–794; for Israel see 830.7

797 Travelers' Accounts, Travel Journals
Divide like 740–794

798 Collective Biography
Biographies may also be classified with specific subjects; use the respective number with 798 or 799 (e.g., 560.799 for biographies of individual authors). For biographies of biblical personalities, see 008; Talmudic personalities, see 103.7

.1	Genealogy; Family Trees
.2	Family Histories
.3	Names of Persons and Places
.4	Epitaphs
.76	Eastern Europe
.765	Western Europe

.77 United States
.8 Israel
.9 Other

799   Individual Biography
See note under 798
.76 Eastern Europe
.765 Western Europe
.77 United States
.8 Israel
.9 Other

800–899

Israel and Zionism

800 **Zionism**
  .4   Dictionaries, Encyclopedias, Directories
  .5   Transactions
  .9   Anti-Zionism
          e.g., American Council for Judaism

801   **Addresses, Essays, Lectures**

802   **Philosophy of Zionism**
  .1   Pre-modern Zionist Thought
  .2   Pre-Herzlian Zionist Theory
  .3   Herzlian "Political" Zionism
  .4   Ahad ha-Am "Cultural" Zionism
  .5   "Practical" Zionism
  .6   Socialist Zionist Thought
  .7   General Zionist Political Theory
  .8   Religious Zionist Thought
  .9   Post-Statehood Zionist Thought

803 Study and Teaching

804 History of Zionism
        Divide like 740–794
.1   Pre-Herzlian Zionism
.2   1897–1948
.3   1948–

805 *National Institutions, Zionist Organizational Structure*
.9   Directories

806 World Zionist Organization
.1   World Zionist Congress
      Including Basle Program
.2   National and Regional Zionist Federations
      e.g., American Zionist Council, British Zionist Federation, Zionist Organization of America
      Divide like 740–794
.3   Zionist Banks
      e.g., Jewish Colonial Trust
.9   Directories

810 *Zionist Parties and Popular Organizations*
.7   History
.8   Non-Party Youth and Student Organizations
      e.g., Student Zionist Organization

811 General Zionism
        For political parties in Israel, see 843
.1   History

.2	Doctrines and Ideologies
.4	General Zionists
.5	Progressives
.6	Hadassah
.7	WIZO
.8	*Hanoar Hatzioni*
.9	Young Judaea

812 Labor Zionism
For political parties in Israel, see **843**

.1	History
.2	Doctrines and Ideologies
.4	*Po'alei Zion*
.5	*Hashomer Ha-zair*
.6	*He-chalutz Ha-zair*
.7	*Habonim*
.8	Pioneer Women

813 Religious Zionism
For political parties in Israel, see **843**

.1	History
.2	Doctrines and Ideologies
.3	*Mizrachi*
.4	*Po'alei Mizrachi*
.5	*Bnei Akiva*

814 Revisionism
For political parties in Israel, see **843**

.1	History
.2	Doctrines and Ideologies
.3	Revisionists
.4	New Revisionists
.5	*Betar*

815 National Institutions

816 Jewish Agency for Israel

817 *Keren Kayemet le-Yisrael* (Jewish National Fund)

818 *Keren Hayesod* (Foundation Fund)

819 Other National Institutions

820 *Israel (Eretz Yisrael)*
.1 Addresses, Lectures
.3 Study and Teaching
.5 Archaeology
.7 General History
.8 Commentaries, Essays, Impressions
.9 Encyclopedias, Dictionaries, Directories

821 Ancient Israel
From the beginning of man's record in the land to the Hebrew settlement

822 Hebrew Settlement to Babylonian Exile
Including material relating to the habitation of the land not otherwise subsumed under *Bible* or *History*

823 Babylonia Exile to Roman Conquest
See note under 822
.1 The Land of Israel under the Persians

.2	The Land of Israel under the Hellenistic Empires
.3	The Land of Israel under the Hasmoneans
.4	Idumea

824	Roman and Byzantine Occupation
	See note under 822
.3	Masada
.5	Nabateans

825	Moslem Conquest to Safed Center (638–c. 1450)
.5	Crusades (1099–1291)

826	Safed Center to Zionist Revival (c. 1450–c. 1840)
	Including history of Israel under the Ottoman Empire

827	Zionist Revival to the Creation of the State
.1	First Settlements (1840–1878)
.2	First Aliyah (1878–1897)
	Including BILU (*Beit Yaakov Lekhu V'Nelkhah*)
.3	Second Aliyah (1893–1913)
.4	World War I and British Occupation (1914–1920)
	Including Zion Mule Corps, Jewish Legion, NILI
.5	Mandatory Palestine (1921–1948)
	Including Haganah, Irgun, Zionist Commission
.6	Third Aliyah (1921–1929)
.7	Fourth Aliyah and Arab Revolt (1930–1939)
	Including the White Paper of 1939

.8 World War II (1939–1945)
.9 The Struggle for Statehood (1946–1948)
Including illegal immigration, UN Partition Resolution (1947)

828 Statehood (1948–)
.1 1948–1955
.13 The War of Independence (1948–1949)
Including Rhodes (Armistice) Agreements
.2 1956–1966
.23 The Sinai Campaign (1956)
.3 1967–1972
.33 The Six Day War (1967)
.4 1973–1981
.43 The Yom Kippur War (1973)
.5 1982–1992
.53 Shalom Ha-Galil Campaign (Lebanon War, 1982)
.54 Intifada
.55 Gulf War (1991)
.6 1993–
Including the Oslo Accords and the Peace Process

830   Israel—Geography
.1 Historical Geography
.2 Social Geography
.3 Economic Geography
.4 Physical Geography
.5 Atlases, Maps
.6 Geographical Place Names
.7 Travel Guides

| 800–899 | 151 |

831 Environment and Natural Resources
.1 Geology
.3 Climate
.5 Flora
.6 Fauna

832 Galilee
Including under this and the other major regional headings (832–839) are optional subheadings that can be used to subdivide the country (*Eretz Yisrael*) regionally so that every city, town (local council), regional council, and settlement—past or present—in Israel may be assigned a specific location in the classification system. Libraries that do not wish to use such a detailed scheme can simply follow the basic regional division adding subheadings for the more important cities.
.1 Upper Galilee
.11 Merom Hagalil Regional Council
.12 Maaleh Hagalil Regional Council
.151 Safed (Zefat)
.18 Minorities' Villages and Settlements
.19 Historic Settlements No Longer Inhabited
.2 Lower Galilee
.21 Hagalil Hatahton Regional Council
.251 Nazareth
.252 Nazerat Illit (Upper Nazareth)
.253 Kefar Tavor
.28 Minorities' Villages and Settlements
.29 Historic Settlements No Longer Inhabited

.3	Western Galilee
.31	Sulam Tzur Regional Council
.32	Ga'aton Regional Council
.33	Na'aman Regional Council
.351	Nahariyya
.352	Ma'alot-Tarshiha
.353	Acre (Akko)
.354	Carmiel
.38	Minorities' Villages and Settlements
.33	Historic Settlements No Longer Inhabited

833   Jordan Valley
See note under **832**

.1	Huleh Valley
.11	Hagalil Haelyon Regional Council
.151	Metullah
.152	Kiryat Shemonah
.153	Hazor
.154	Rosh Pinnah
.155	Yesud Hama'alah
.18	Minorities' Villages and Settlements
.19	Historic Settlements No Longer Inhabited
.2	Sea of Galilee (Lake Kinneret) and Kinneret Valley
.21	Emek Hayarden Regional Council
.211	Deganyah
.251	Tiberias (Teveryah)
.252	Kinneret
.28	Minorities' Villages and Settlements
.29	Historic Settlements No Longer Inhabited
.291	Capernaum (Kfar Nahum)

.3	Beit She'an (Beisan) Valley
.31	Bika'at Bet She'an Regional Council
.351	Bet She'an
.352	Menahemia
.38	Minorities' Villages and Settlements
.39	Historic Settlements No Longer Inhabited
.4	Lower Jordan Valley
.48	Minorities' Villages and Settlements
.481	Jericho
.49	Historic Settlements No Longer Inhabited
.5	Dead Sea (Yam ha-Melah)
.59	Historical Settlements No Longer Inhabited

834 Jezreel Valley (Emek Yizre'el)
See note under 832

.1	Mount Tabor
.11	Yizre'el Regional Council
.12	Hagilboa Regional Council
.15	Afula
.18	Minorities' Villages and Settlements
.19	Historic Settlements No Longer Inhabited
.2	Kishon Valley
.21	Kishon Regional Council
.251	Migdal Ha-Emek
.28	Minorities' Villages and Settlements
.29	Historic Settlements No Longer Inhabited

835 Samaria (Shomron)
See note under 832

.1	Ephraim (Samarian Hills)

.12	Ashdot Shomron Regional Council
.121	Ariel
.122	Elkanah
.123	Karnei Shomron
.124	Kedumim
.129	Other Jewish Settlements
.13	Matteh Binyamin Regional Council
.131	Bet El
.18	Minorities' Villages and Settlements
.181	Shechem (Nablus)
.182	Jenin
.183	Tulkarem
.19	Historic Settlements No Longer Inhabited
.2	Menasheh (Manasseh) Hills
.21	Megiddo Regional Council
.251	Kiryat Tivon
.252	Kiryat Haroshet
.253	Yokne'am
.28	Minorities' Villages and Settlements
.29	Historic Settlements No Longer Inhabited
.3	Shefelat Hashomron
.31	Modi'in Regional Council
.32	Gezer Regional Council
.351	Lod (Lydda)
.352	Ramleh
.353	Kiryat Ekron
.38	Minorities' Villages and Settlements
.39	Historic Settlements No Longer Inhabited

836 Coastal Plain
See note under 832

.1 Emek Zevulun (Haifa Bay) and Haifa Metropolitan Region
.11 Zevulun Regional Council
.14 Haifa
.152 Kiryat Yam
.153 Kiryat Bialik
.154 Kiryat Ata
.155 Kiryat Motzkin
.156 Nesher
.157 Tirat Karmel
.18 Minorities' Villages and Settlements
.19 Historical Settlements No Longer Inhabited

.2 Mount Carmel
.21 Hof Hacarmel Regional Council
.22 Alonah Regional Council
.23 Menasheh Regional Council
.28 Minorities' Villages and Settlements
.29 Historic Settlements No Longer Inhabited

.3 Emek Hefer
.31 Emek Hefer Regional Council
.351 Zikhron Ya'akov
.352 Giv'at Adah
.353 Binyaminah
.38 Minorities' Villages and Settlements
.39 Historic Settlements No Longer Inhabited

.4 Sharon Plains
.41 Hasharon Hatzefoni Regional Council
.42 Hadar Hasharon Regional Council

.43	Hof Hasharon Regional Council
.44	Hasharon Hatichon Regional Council
.451	Or Akiva
.452	Pardes Hannah-Karkur
.453	Haderah
.454	Netanyah
.455	Kefar Yonah
.456	Pardesiyah
.457	Even Yehudah
.458	Tel Mond
.461	Kefar Saba
.462	Ra'anannah
.463	Ramat Hashavim
.464	Hod Ha-Sharon
.48	Minorities' Villages and Settlements
.49	Historic Settlements No Longer Inhabited
.6	Dan Region (Tel Aviv-Yafo Metropolitan Region)
.61	Ono Regional Council
.62	Hayarkon Regional Council
.63	Mifalot Efek Regional Council
.64	Tel Aviv-Jaffa (Yafo)
.651	Kfar Shemaryahu
.652	Herzliyah
.653	Ramat Ha-Sharon
.654	Bene-Berak
.655	Ramat Gan
.656	Givatayim
.657	Petah Tikvah
.658	Gannei Tikvah
.659	Kiryat Shmuel
.661	Kiryat Ono
.662	Yahud

.663	Or Yehudah
.664	Azor
.665	Neveh Efrayim (Monosson)
.666	Savyon
.667	Bet Dagan
.668	Holon
.669	Bat Yam
.68	Minorities' Villages and Settlements
.69	Historic Settlements No Longer Inhabited
.7	Central Coast
.71	Emek Lod Regional Council
.72	Gan Ravek Regional Council
.73	Brener Regional Council
.74	Hevel Yavneh Regional Council
.751	Nahalat Yehudah
.752	Rishon Le-Zion
.753	Nes Ziyona
.754	Be'er Ya'akov
.755	Rehovot
.756	Yavneh
.78	Minorities' Villages and Settlements
.79	Historic Settlements No Longer Inhabited
.8	Judean Coast
.81	Beer Tuvia Regional Council
.82	Shafir Regional Council
.83	Nof Ashkelon Regional Council
.84	Shaar Hanegev Regional Council
.851	Gederah
.852	Gan Yavneh
.853	Ashdod
.854	Kiryat Malakhi

.855 Ashkelon
.88 Minorities' Villages and Settlements
.89 Historic Settlements No Longer Inhabited

837 Judea
    See note under **832**
.1 Judean Hills
.11 Mateh Yehudah Regional Council
.14 Jerusalem
.145 Western Wall
.151 Bet(h) Shemesh
.152 Mevasseret Zion
.161 Ma'aleh Adummim
.162 Efrat
.163 Kiryat Arba
    Including Jewish Settlement in Hebron
.164 Ofrah
.165 Tekoa
.166 Ezyon Bloc
.18 Minorities' Villages and Settlements
.181 Bethlehem
.182 Hebron
.183 Ramallah
.184 Bir Zeit
.19 Historic Settlements No Longer Inhabited

.2 Judean Desert
.251 Arad
.28 Minorities' Villages and Settlements
.29 Historic Settlements No Longer Inhabited

.3 Shefelat Yehudah
.31 Yoav Regional Council

.32	Lachish Regional Council
.351	Kiryat Gat
.38	Minorities' Villages and Settlements
.39	Historic Settlements No Longer Inhabited

838 Negev

.1	Beersheba Valley (Northern Negev)
.11	Shelachim Regional Council
.12	Azata Regional Council
.13	Merhavim Regional Council
.14	B'nei Shimon Regional Council
.15	Hevel Ma'on Regional Council
.151	Beersheba (Be'er Sheva)
.152	Sederot
.153	Netivot
.154	Ofakim
.17	Jewish Settlements in the Gaza Strip
.18	Minorities' Villages and Settlements
.181	Gaza
.182	Khan Yunis
.183	Rafiah
.19	Historic Settlements No Longer Inhabited
.2	Ramat Hanegev
.21	Ramat Hanegev Regional Council
.22	Tamar Regional Council
.251	Dimonah
.252	Yeroham
.253	Mizpeh Ramon
.28	Minorities' Villages and Settlements
.29	Historic Settlements No Longer Inhabited

.3	Southern Negev
.31	Hevel Eilot Regional Council
.351	Eilat
.38	Minorities' Villages and Settlements
.39	Historic Settlements No Longer Inhabited
.5	Sinai Peninsula
.59	Historic Settlements No Longer Inhabited

839 Transjordan
See note under 832

.1	Edom
.2	Moab
.3	Ammon
.4	Gilead
.5	Golan Heights
.51	Kazrin
.59	Historic Settlements No Longer Inhabited

840 Israel—Government and Politics

.1	Addresses, Essays, Lectures
.2	Political Theory
.3	Study and Teaching
.4	Dictionaries and Encyclopedias
.5	Transactions, Directories
.7	History

841 Constitution, Constitutional Law

.1 The "Little Constitution" and Basic Law of the State

> The special constitutional legislation of the *Knesset* and materials relating to it

.2	Constitutional Development and Interpretation
.9	Proposed Constitutions

842 Political Participation, Elections, Electoral Behavioral
- .1 Citizenship and Suffrage
- .2 Election Laws, Conduct of Elections
- .3 Voting Behavior
- .4 Public Opinion
- .5 Political Campaigning
- .6 Pressure or Lobby Groups
  e.g., Black Panthers, Peace Now, Gush Emunim

843 Party System, Parties
Including general material on parties, past and present, and material on specific parties
- .1 "Labor Camp"
  e.g., *Mapai, Mapam*, Labor Movement
- .2 "National (Civil) Camp"
  e.g., *Herut*, Likud
- .3 "Religious Camp"
  e.g., Agudat Israel, National Religious Party
- .4 Non-Zionist Parties
  e.g., Communist

844 Legislative Process, Knesset (Parliament)
- .4 Directories
- .5 Knesset Debates
- .6 Committees

845 Executive, President and Cabinet, Public Administration
- .1 President and Office of the President

.2 Cabinet
.3 Prime Minister and the Office of Prime Minister

846 **Public Finance, Fiscal Affairs**
.1 Taxation
.2 Budgeting

847 **Public Administration**
.1 Civil Service
.2 State Comptroller
.3 Ombudsman (*Natziv Telunot Hatzibbun*)

848 **Foreign Relations**
> For relations with governments of specific countries, divide like 750–794. For relations with the countries of the Middle East, see 890–899

.3 Anti-Israel Propaganda
.4 Economic Assistance to Other Nations
.6 Israel and the European Community
.7 Israel–U.S. Relations
.95 Israel and the United Nations

849 **Defense, Military Affairs**
.4 Intelligence and Security
.5 Army
.6 Air Force
.7 Navy
.8 Nahal
.9 Military Courts

850 **Judiciary, Courts**
> For religious courts, see 852; military courts, see 849.9

	.1	Supreme Court
	.2	Other Civil Courts
		Magistrates' courts, district courts, municipal courts, juvenile courts, etc.
	.5	Civil Rights

851 Civil and Criminal Law
  e.g., Adoption, capital punishment, discrimination
  .1 Influence of Jewish Law

852 Religious Law and Courts
  For religious organization in Israel, see **876**
  .1 Jewish
  .2 Muslim
  .3 Christian
  .4 Druze

853 Law Enforcement

854 Local Government
  .1 Municipalities
  .2 Local Councils
  .3 Regional Councils
  .4 Central-Local Relations

855 Israel—Economics and Development

856 Planning
  .3 Housing

857 Land Use, Conservation, Reclamation, Ecology
.1 Water Resources, Irrigation
.2 Reforestation
.3 Parks
.4 Ecology

858 Agriculture and Settlement
Including material on forms of settlement
For material on organizations assisting settlement, e.g., Jewish Agency, Jewish National Fund, see 816, 817
.2 Animal Husbandry
.3 Agricultural Research
.4 Agricultural Cooperatives
For other cooperative movements, see 863.2
.5 Moshava
.6 Kevutza and Kibbutz
.7 Moshav Ovdim and Moshav Shittufi
.8 Plantations, Private Farms, and Groves
.9 Rural Agricultural Workers' Settlements

859 Banking, Finance, and Investment
Including overseas investments in Israel

860 Commerce and Commercial Development, Trade
.1 Standards, Weights and Measures
.2 Public Utilities
.3 Merchandising
.9 Foreign Trade

861	**Manufacturing and Industry**
.1	Mining
.2	Fishing
.3	Oil and Gas
.4	Construction
862	**Transportation and Communications**
.1	Railroads
.2	Airlines
.3	Highways, Intercity buses
.4	Ocean Travel, Shipping
.5	Local Transit
.6	Postal Service
.7	Telephone and Telegraph
863	**Labor and Labor Organizations**
.1	Histadrut
.2	Cooperative Movements
.3	Working Conditions
.4	Labor Relations
864	**Science and Technology**

865 Israel—Demography, Population

Vital statistics; births and birth rates, marriage and divorce, etc.

866 Characteristics of the Jewish Population

Including materials on countries of origin, health and disease patterns, physiological changes, etc.

.4 Youth, Youth Movements
.619 Women

867 Characteristics of Non-Jewish Population
- .1 Arab
- .2 Druze
- .3 Circassian
- .5 Other
- .6 Youth, Youth Movements

868 Immigration
Source, conditions, methods, statistics, refugees, Youth Aliyah
For history, see 827
- .1 *Kibbutz Galuyyot* (Idea of the Ingathering of Exiles into Israel)
- .5 Absorption of Immigrants
- .9 Emigration (*Yerida*)

869 Social Conditions and Problems
e.g., integration of "communities" of Jews living in Israel (*eydot*), juvenile delinquency, family life, etc.

870 Social Welfare
e.g., adoption
- .1 Children

871 Health and Medical Services
- .5 *Kuppat Holim*
- .7 *Magen David Adom* (Israeli "Red Cross")

872 General Education
- .1 State Schools
- .2 State Religious Schools

.3 Private Schools and *Yeshivot*
.4 Vocational Schools
.5 "Minorities" Schools
.6 Special Schools
    e.g., ulpan

873 Higher Education
.1 Hebrew University
.2 Technion, Israel Institute of Technology
.3 Weizmann Institute of Science
.4 Tel Aviv University
.5 Haifa University
.6 Bar-Ilan University
.7 Ben Gurion University
.8 Colleges and Teacher
.9 Other

874 Libraries
.1 Jewish National and University Library
.5 Archives
.6 Zionist Archives
.8 Museums
.9 Israel National Museum

875 Israel—Culture

876 Religion, Religious Organization
    For Religious Zionism, see 813; for Religious Parties, see 843.3; for Religious Courts, see 852; for Religious Kibbutzim, see 858.6
.1 Relations with the State

.2   Orthodox Religious Movements and Organizations
        Non-Zionist movements and non-Zionist aspects of religious organizations, e.g., *Neturei Karta*, *Agudat Israel*
.3   Liberal Religious Movements and Organizations
        e.g., Reform, Progressives
.4   The Rabbinate
.6   Minority Religions
        Including Christian missions

877   Celebrations, National Observances
        For celebration of Jewish holidays in the traditional manner, see 235–265; for general material on celebrating Yom Ha-Atzma'ut, see 259

878   The Press, Publishing, Mass Media
        For issues of specific periodicals, see 922
.5   Radio and Television
        Including *Kol Yisrael*

879   Sports and Recreation

880   *Israel—Arts*

881   Architecture and Structural Design

882   Music and Dance

883   Theater
.1   *Habimah*

884 Graphic and Plastic Arts

885 Israel and World Jewry
For relations with individual Diaspora communities, divide like 740–794; e.g., 885.7 Israel–U.S. Jewish community relations

886 Political Relations and Problems
See note under 885

887 Educational and Cultural Relations
See note under 885

888 Religious Relations and Problems
See note under 885

889 Economic Relations
See note under 885

890 Israel and the Middle East
.5   Israel-Arab Relations
.51   Peace Efforts and Negotiations
       Including peace treaties with Arab states
.55   Arab Boycott
.6   Israel and the Palestinian Arabs
       Including the Palestinian Authority
.61   Terrorism and Terrorist Organizations
       Including the Palestine Liberation Organization
.62   Counter-terrorism
.7   Arab Refugees
.9   Special Topics

891		Middle East
		Including general and political works on the Arabs; for specific countries, use 892–899. For Jews in the following countries, use 740–760
	.2	Geography
	.4	Social Characteristics, Anthropology
	.5	Government and Politics
	.6	Economics
	.7	History
892		Jordan
893		Egypt (and United Arab Republic)
894		Syria and Lebanon
895		Saudi Arabia
896		Iraq
897		Iran
898		Turkey
899		Other Middle Eastern States
	.1	Sudan
	.2	Libya
	.3	Cyprus
	.4	Aden
	.5	Yemen
	.6	Afghanistan

900–999

General Works

900 **Jewish Encyclopedias**
Encyclopedias covering the range of Jewish subjects, e.g., Encyclopaedia Judaica, Junior Judaica

901 General Encyclopedias
e.g., Britannica, World Book

902 Encyclopedias/Dictionaries of Religion
General in scope. Single subject encyclopedias should be classified with their appropriate subjects

903 Encyclopedias/Dictionaries of General Philosophy

904 Encyclopedias/Dictionaries of General Languages
> Including general language dictionaries, e.g., Webster's

905 Encyclopedias/Dictionaries of General Literature

906 Encyclopedias/Dictionaries of the Social Sciences

907 Encyclopedias/Dictionaries of General History, Universal Histories

908 General Atlases, Gazetteers, Geographic Encyclopedias

909 General Yearbooks/Almanacs

910 General Collections of Essays on Jewish Topics
> Collections of general essays, addresses, lectures by one or more authors; collections of non-literary essays; festschriften

915–919 Jewish Yearbooks, Almanacs, Directories
> General popular works. Those dealing with single subjects may be classified with the subject

915	Israel
.8	Middle East

916	United States
	e.g., *American Jewish Yearbook*

917	Great Britain

918	Other Countries
	Divide like 740–794

919	International Jewish Organizations

920 Jewish Journalism
.3	Addresses, Essays, and Lectures
.6	Associations, Directories, and Societies
.7	History
	Divide like 740–794

921	General Jewish Periodicals (Newspapers and Magazines)
	Including works about periodicals and their use, general indexes to periodicals, and individual periodicals
.3	Indexes, Reader's Guides
.6	Directories
.9	Press Services
	e.g., Jewish Telegraphic Agency

922	Israeli Periodicals

923	American Jewish Periodicals

924	British Jewish Periodicals
925	Other Periodicals *Divide like 740–794*
930	General Jewish Societies—Proceedings, Transactions Regularly issued proceedings and transactions of learned societies

940 *The Jewish Book*
Including history of Jewish books and bookmaking

.1	Copyright
.3	Braille Publications
941	History of Jewish Printing and Publishing Houses e.g., Jewish Publication Society of America
.6	Directories Including both Jewish and general publishing houses
942	Manuscripts Rare handwritten volumes, primarily from before the invention of printing
.1	Bible
.2	Classical Judaica: Halakhah and Midrash
.3	Jewish Observance and Practice
.4	Education
.5	Hebrew, Jewish Languages, and Sciences
.6	Literature

.7	Jewish Life and Arts
.8	History and Biography
.9	Israel

943 Incunabula
Divide like 942

944 Rare Printing, Special Editions
Divide like 942

945 Rare Bindings
Divide like 942

946 Rare Illustrations
Divide like 942

947 Book Plates
Divide like 942

948 Other Rare Characteristics
Divide like 942

949 Other Rare Materials
Divide like 942

950-959   Jewish Bibliography
Bibliographies may also be classified with specific subject area with .95

950 Bible

951 Classical Judaica: Halakhah and Midrash

952   Jewish Observance and Practice

953   Jewish Education

954   Hebrew, Jewish Languages, and Sciences

955   Jewish Literature
   .1   Juvenile
                Including suggestion for the use of books

956   The Jewish Community: Society and the Arts

957   Jewish History and Biography

958   Israel and Zionism

959   General Jewish Bibliographies
                Including union catalogs and book catalogs of individual libraries
   .5   Bibliography of Bibliographies
   .6   Publishers' Catalogs
   .7   History of Jewish Bibliography

960 *Audiovisual Materials*
To be used for classifying the actual materials. Audiovisual materials may also be classified in specific subject areas with prefixes to denote type

For information on the role and use of audiovisual materials in education, see **328.1**
   .1   Manuals
   .9   Bibliographies

| 961 | Movies; Video Cassettes
Divide like 942 |

| 962 | Filmstrips
Divide like 942 |

| 963 | Slides
Divide like 942 |

| 964 | Records
Divide like 942 |

| 965 | Audio Tapes, CDs
Divide like 942 |

| 966 | Flashcards, Flannelboards
Divide like 942 |

| 967 | Maps, Charts
Teaching maps only
Divide like 942 |

| 968 | Computer Software
Including all formats (tapes, diskettes, CD-ROM)
For library automation see 970.4
Divide like 942 |

| 969 | Pictures
Divide like 942 |

970 Library Science

- .4 Library Automation
  Including computer software for library automation
- .7 History
- .9 Directories

971 Library Organization and Administration

- .1 The School Library
- .2 The University Library
- .5 Copyright

972 The Book Collection
Including book selection

973 Classification
Including classification schedules, e.g., Dewey, Library of Congress

974 Circulation

975 Cataloging
Including subject headings

976 Reference

- .1 Online Searching
  Including Internet, Compuserve, World Wide Web, Dialog, etc.

977 Juvenile

978 Buildings and Facilities

979	Archives

980 The Jewish Library
Divide like 740–794; for libraries in Israel, see 874

.1 Association, Directories, and Societies
.2 Addresses, Essays, Lectures
.3 Organization and Administration

982 The Book Collection
Including book selection

983 Classification
Including classification schedules
e.g., Elazar, Weine

984 Cataloging
Including subject headings

985 Reference
.1 Online Searching
Including Internet, Compuserve, World Wide Web, Dialog, etc.

986 Juvenile

987 The School Library

988 Special Libraries

989 Jewish Archives
.1 Oral History

995 The Jewish Museum
Divide like 740–794; for museums in Israel, see 874.8
- .1 Associations, Directories, and Societies
- .2 Addresses, Essays, and Lectures
- .3 Organization and Administration

996 Museumology

997 Museum Technology

998 Exhibits and Displays

999 Buildings and Equipment

Index

Abbreviations (*rashe tevot*)
   Hebrew language   401.6
Abortion   651.5
Academy of the Hebrew Language, *see Vaad Ha-Lashon Ha-Ivrit*
Adloyada (Purim carnival)   249.8
Adolescence   397.23
Adoption   652.4
   in Israel
      civil law   851
      social welfare   870
   in Jewish law
      Codes   125.4
      Responsa   125.5
Adult education   375
Adultery   652.5
   in Israel
      criminal law   851
   in Jewish law
      Bible   011.1
      Codes   125.4
      Responsa   125.5
      Talmud   101.9

Africa (not including North Africa)
   Jews in   790
Afterlife, see *Olam ha-ba*
Afula   834.15
Aged, services for   638.3
Aggadah-Classical Midrash   140
   Biblical Midrashim   141
   Ethical Midrashim   142
   Festival Midrashim (*Pesiktot*)   143
   Historical Midrashim   144
   Post-Classical Midrashim   145
Aging (social condition)   653
Agnosticism   136.38
Agriculture
   as a Jewish occupation   647.1
   in Israel   858
Agudat Israel
   political party   843.3
   religious movement   876.2
Aharonim   130
   Codes   130.4
   Responsa   130.5
Air Force, Israeli   849.6
Alchemy   164.5
Alcoholism   656.5
Aliyah
   First (1878–1897)   827.2
   Fourth (1930–1939)   827.7
   illegal immigration (1946–1948)   827.9
   Second (1898–1913)   827.3
   Third (1921–1929)   827.6
   to Israel   868
   Torah reading   224

Index

Alliance Israelite Universelle	644.9
Almanacs	915–919
Alphabets	
Aramaic	417
Hebrew	401
Ladino	427
Yiddish	437
American Council for Judaism	800.9
American Jewish Committee	637.7
American Jewish Congress	637.7
American Jewry, see	
Canada, Jews in	
Latin America, Jews in	
South America, Jews in	
U.S., Jews in	
American Zionist Council	806.27
Amoraim	120
Amoraitic Period (historical c.200–500 CE)	728
Amos	040
Amulets	
Kabbalah	150.9
Numismatics	676
Ancient Near East, see Near East, Ancient	
Anthologies	
Aggadah	135.5
Bible	003.9
Jewish literature	550
Talmud	101.2
Zohar	159.5
Anthropomorphism	136.18
Anti-Defamation League	637.7
Anti-Semitism	662
Anti-Zionism	800.9

Apikoros (agnosticism)	136.38
Apocrypha	070
Apologetics, Christian	662.95
Apostasy	661.9
Arab boycott	890.55
Arab-Israel relations	890.5
Peace efforts and negotiations	890.51
Arab refugees	890.7
Arab revolt	827.7
Arab terrorism	890.61
Arabs	
folklore	195.2
Israeli	867.1
language	461
literature	592
Middle Eastern	891
Palestinian	890.6
refugees	890.7
relations with Israel	890.5
relations with Jews	661.5
Arad	837.251
Aramaic language	415
Archeology	
Biblical	010
in Israel	820.5
Near East, Ancient	091
Architecture	671
civic	673
in Israel	881
synagogue	672
Archives	640.3
in Israel	874.5

Index

organization	979, 989
Zionist	874.6
Aristeas, Letter of	085.1
Ark, *see* Aron Kodesh	
Ark of the Covenant, *see* Aron Ha-brit	
Armed Forces, Jews in	
Biblical period	007
Israel	849
Armenia, Jews in	764.5
Aron ha-Brit	006.5
Aron Kodesh	224
Art	670
education	339.1
Artisans (as an occupation)	647.2
Asarah B'Tevet (10th of Tevet)	255
Aseret ha-Dibbrot (Ten Commandments)	021
Aseret Yomei Teshuvah (10 days of repentance)	238
Ashdod	836.853
Ashkelon	836.855
Ashkenazic Jewry	
cooking and culinary arts	699.2
customs (social)	610
ethnography	603
history	760
language (Yiddish)	435
literature	503
anthologies	553
liturgy	232
social history	601
Asia	
Jews in	792
Assimilation	655.5

Astrology	
Bible	012.2
Astronomy	
Bible	012.2
science	482
Talmud	101.9
Atheism	136.39
Atlases	908
Israel	830.5
Atonement (*Kapparah*)	136.57
Audiovisual	
classification	960–969
education	328.1
Auschwitz (concentration camp)	736.1
Australia, Jews in	794.1
Austria, Jews in	762.4
Autobiographies	799
Autonomy	
community structure and government	620
Kehillot	623
Avot, Masekhet (*Pirke Avot*)	107.12
Ba'alei Teshuvah Movement	214.5
Babylonian exile	
biblical history	007.6
historical period	719
Babylonian Talmud	101
Balfour Declaration	827.4
Banking (including moneylending)	
as a Jewish occupation	647.3
in Israel	859
Zionist Banks	806.3
Bar Kokhba Revolt	727.5

Index

Bar Mitzvah	222.3
Baraita (Tannaitic writings not included in the Mishnah)	113
Basle Program	806.1
Bat Mitzvah	222.31
Bathing	
customs	612
hygiene	612
ritual (*mikveh*)	221.5
Bedikat Hametz	244.11
Beersheba	838.151
Beit Shean	833.351
Belarus, Jews in	764.3
Belgium, Jews in	768.2
Bene-Berak	836.654
Bene-Israel (India Jewry)	792.1
in Israel	866
liturgy	233
Benedictions	230.9
Berakhot (Blessings)	230.91
Bet Din	625
Rabbinical courts in Israel	852
Beta Yisrael (Ethiopian Jews)	790.1
customs (Social)	610
literature	502
liturgy	233
Bet(h) Shemesh	837.151
Bethlehem	837.181
Bible (Tanakh; for Christian Scriptures, *see* 292.1)	001
abridgements, selections	003.9
archeology	010
biography	008
commentaries	002

Bible (*continued*)	
concordances	003.5
criticism	005
dictionaries	003.4
environment	009
essays	014
history	007
impact	013
institutions	006
linguistics	004
literature	011.5
polyglot	001.5
research	005
special topics	012
study aids	003
translation from Hebrew	001.2
Bibliography (books)	950–959
of bibliographies	959.5
Bikkur Holim (visit to the sick)	136.75
BILU (*Bet Yaakov Lekhu Ve-nelkhah*)	827.2
Biographies (including autobiographies)	
Bible	008
collective	
Israel	798.8
U.S.	798.7
individual	
Israel	799.8
U.S.	799.7
Talmud	103.7
Biological characteristics of the Jews	602
Birkat ha-Hodesh (Blessing of the New Moon)	265
Birth	
birth rates in Israel	865

Index

customs	611
religious rites	222
Birth control	
ethics (social)	652.3
in Jewish law	
Bible	012
Codes	125.4
Responsa	125.5
Talmud	101.9
Black-Jewish relations	661.7
Black Jews, see also Beta Yisrael	603
Blessings, see Berakhot	
Blood libel, see Anti-Semitism	
B'nai Akiva	813.5
Bnei Brith	639.7
Board of Deputies of British Jews	622.9
Book plates	947
Books, Jewish	940
bibliography	950–959
classification	973, 983
history of printing and publishing	941
Botany	
Bible	009.3
Boycott, Arab, see Arab Boycott	
Braille	
publications	940.3
study and teaching	386
Bread	
blessing	230.9
cookery	699.9
hallah (Sabbath bread)	237.1
Brigade, Jewish, see Jewish Brigade	
Brit Milah (Circumcision)	222.1

British Jewry, *see* England, Jews in
British Zionist Federation   806.266
Brotherhoods (Synagogue)   636.3
Bund, Jewish   648.3
Burial
    customs   613
    places, *see* cemeteries
    rites, *see* Funeral Rites
    societies (*Hevra Kaddisha*)   638.7
Burma, Jews in   792.4

Cabalah, *see* Kabbalah
Calendar   235
    comprehensive   235.1
    history   235.7
Calligraphy   681.5
Camps and camping   381
    day camps   381.1
    directories   381.4
    Hebrew speaking   381.2
    Zionist camps   381.3
Canaanites   095.71
Canada, Jews in   784
    literature   521
Canadian Jewish Congress   622.9
Cantatas   688
    sacred music   686.5
Cantillation   686.1
Cantor, *see* Hazan
Capernaum (Kfar Nahum)   833.291
Capital punishment
    in Israel
       criminal law   851

in Jewish law	
Bible	012
Codes	125.4
Responsa	125.5
Talmud	101.9
Capitalism	665
Caribbean, Jews in	786
Carmel (Mt.)	836.2
Cataloging (books)	975, 984
Catholic Church and the Jews	661.3
CD-ROM	968
Cemeteries	
architecture	673.5
burial customs	613
burial services (*Hevra Kaddisha*)	638.7
religious rites	222.5
Censorship	630
Census	
Israel	865
reports	606
Central America, Jews in	787
Central Asian Republics, Jews in	764.2
Ceramic arts	677
Ceremonial art	674
Chanukah, *see* Hanukkah	
Chaplains	638.8
Charity	
concept, *see* Tzedakah	
operation, *see* Fund-raising	
Chelm stories	190.3
Child Abuse	397.5
Child development	
adolescence	397.23

Child development (*continued*)
  elementary   397.22
  infant and pre-school   397.21
Children
  education   305
    Israel   872
  family relations   652
  Jewish education   300
    curriculum   330
    Israel   308
  juvenile delinquency   654
    Israel   869
  psychology   397
Children's
  cookbooks   699.4
  games   696
  literature   986
  songs   687.11
China, Jews in   792.2
Choirs and choral music
  sacred   686.3
Chosen People Concept   136.81
Christ, *see* Jesus
Christian-Jewish relations   661.3
Christian scriptures   292.1
Christianity   292
  and anti-semitism   662
Chronicles
  I (*Divrei ha-Yamim Alef*)   068
  II (*Divrei ha-Yamim Bet*)   069
Chronology   705
Circumcision, *see* Brit Milah

Index

Citizenship (Jewish Community)	629
Israel	842.1
Civil rights	
in Israel	850.5
Jews in world order	667
within Jewish community	630
Civil service	
in Israel	847.1
Classical literature	
Jews in	591
Coastal Plain (Israel)	836
Codes	125.4
see also individual codes, i.e., Mishneh Torah	
Coins	676
Collected works, see Anthologies	
Colleges	
administration	367
curriculum	366
institutions	640
publications	369
Commandments, see Taryag Mitzvot	
Commentaries	
Bible	
classic	002
contemporary in traditional vein	002.1
current basic	002.2
history	002.7
non-Jewish	002.8
non-traditional	005
scientific approach	002.3
Mishnah	110.2
Talmud	
classical	101.3

Commentaries (*continued*)
    contemporary in traditional vein   101.5
    current basic   101.4
    Hiddushim (Novellae)   101.6
    Jerusalem   115.2
    non-Jewish   101.8
    traditional   101
Commerce
  as a Jewish occupation   647.3
  in Israel   860
Commonwealth
  first   715
  second   721
Communism   665
Communist Party (Israel)   843.4
Community, Jewish, *see* Jewish Community
Community centers   639
Community councils   624
Community relations   634
Computer Science and programs   489.8
Computer software   968
Concentration camps   736.1
Concerts   694
Concordances
  Bible   003.5
  Mishnah   111.4
  Talmud   102.6
  Torah   017.5
Conduct of life, *see* Ethics
Confirmation   224.91
Conservation   659
Conservative Movement in Judaism   215
  liturgy   232
  thought   178

Index

Constitutional law in Israel	841
Conversion to Judaism	203.8
history	207.9
Conversation manuals, Hebrew	409
Converts from Judaism, *see* Apostasy	
Cookery and culinary arts	699
Cooperative (Agricultural)	
in Israel	858.4
Copyright	971.5
Cosmology	136.2
Costume	617
Counting of the Omer, *see* Sefirat ha-Omer	
Courts	
community	625
Israel	850
military	849.9
religious	852
Covenant	
in Bible	011
in Jewish Law	125.9
in Jewish Thought	136
in Talmud	101.9
with God	136.31
Craftsmen (as an occupation)	647.2
Creation	020.9
Crime	654
in Israel	869
Jewish response to	667
Criticism	
Bible	005
literary	530
Croatia, Jews in	757.72

Crusades	730
in *Eretz Yisrael* (Palestine)	825.5
Cults	661.91
Cultural institutions and organizations	642
Culture	
arts	670
in Israel	875
Curriculum (education)	330
Customs and ceremonies	221
Czech Republic, Jews in	762.3
Damascus Affair	662.54
Dance	695
in Israel	882
Dances	695
interpretive dance	695.2
Israeli folk dances	695.3
Jewish folk dances	695.3
Day camps	381.1
Day schools	313.1
Dead Sea	833.5
Dead Sea Scrolls	010.5
Death and Mourning	010.5
customs	613
religious rites	222.5
Decalogue, *see Aseret ha-Dibbrot*	
Dedication of the home, *see Hanukkat Habayit*	
Deganyah	833.211
Democracy	
Biblical impact on	013.5
in Israel	840
in the Jewish community	620

Index

Demography	606
Israel	865
Denmark, Jews in	769.3
Deuteronomy (Book of the Bible)	024
Dialects	
Judeo-Arabic	447
Judeo-Aramaic	415
Judeo-Greek	448
Judeo-Persian	446
Ladino (Judaeo-Spanish)	425
Yiddish	435
Diaries	799
Diaspora Jewry, see *Galut*	
Dictionaries, see also Encyclopedias	
art	670.4
Biblical	003.4
language	004.4
education	305.4
Hebrew language	403
history	704
holidays and festivals	236.4
language	904
literary	541
Mishnah	111.4
religion	
comparative	290.91
Jewish	207
social history	600.4
Zionism	800.4
Dietary laws, see *Kashrut*	
Directories	915–919
Discrimination	
anti-semitism	662

Discrimination (*continued*)	
in Israel	
civil law	851
civil rights	850.5
social conditions and problems	869
within the Jewish community	630
Divorce	652.1
in Israel	
civil law	851
statistics	865
in Jewish law	
Bible	001
Codes	125.4
Responsa	125.5
Talmud	101
religious rites	222.4
statistics (World Jewry)	606
Drama	
anthologies	550.2
individual works	562
study and teaching	339.2
Dramatic art	691
in Israel	883
music	688
plays	691.1
theater	691
writing	
rhetoric	501.2
Drawing and painting	681
Dress	617
Druse in Israel	867.2

Index

Early childhood education
  curriculum — 332
  methodology — 340
East European Jewry
  customs (social) — 610
  ethnography — 603
  history — 763
  language (Yiddish) — 435
  literature — 503, 504, 553, 554
  liturgy — 232
  social history — 601
Ecclesiastes (Kohelet) — 063
Ecology — 659
  in Israel — 857.4
  in the Bible — 009.5
Economic assistance
  Israel to other nations — 848.4
  within Jewish community — 638.6
Economic conditions
  in Israel — 855
  of the Jews — 646
Education, general — 305
  as an occupation — 647.8
  directories — 305.6
  history — 305.7
  in Israel — 872
  philosophy — 305.1
Education, Jewish — 300
  adult — 375
  associations — 300.6
  directories — 300.6
  early childhood, see Early childhood education

Education, Jewish (*continued*)
  elementary, *see* Elementary education
  extracurricular activities   351
  higher   365
  history   307
  in Israel   308
  intermediate, *see* Elementary education
  philosophy   301
  secondary, *see* Secondary education
  in U.S.   310
  yearbooks   300.9
Educational institutions   640
Egypt
  ancient   093
  Jews in   751
  general   893
Eichmann trial   736.3
Eilat   838.351
Ein Ya'akov   145.5
Election of Israel, *see* Chosen People Concept
Elementary education   345
  curriculum   333
Emancipation of the Jews   734
Emek Yizra'el (Valley of Jezreel)   834
Emigration, *see* Immigration and emigration, Migrations
Emigration from Israel   868.9
Encyclopedias
  general   901
  Jewish   900
  see also subject
Engineering and electronics   489

England
  Jews in
    history   766
    literature   522
  relations with Israel   848.66
    pre-State   827.4
Engraving   682
Enlightenment (historical period), see Haskalah
Entertainment, public   690
Epitaphs   798.4
Equality (civil rights), see Discrimination
Eretz Yisrael, see also Israel (State)
  ancient   821
  Babylonian exile   823
  Byzantine occupation   824
  Hebrew settlement   822
  Hellenistic period   823.2
  history   820.7
  Mandatory Palestine   827.5
  Moslem conquest   825
  Roman conquest   824
  Zionist revival   827
Eretz Yisrael (Concept)   136.85
Eschatology   136.9
Essays
  collections   550.4
  criticism   534
  history and development   500.4
    Hebrew   510.4
    Ladino   501.4
    Yiddish   503.4
  individual works   564
  see also specific literature

Essenes	725.3
Estonia, Jews in	763.5
Ethical wills	500.6, 566
Ethics	136.75
Ethics of the Fathers, see Pirkei Avot	
Ethiopia, Jews in	790.1
Ethnography	603
Etiquette	616
Etrog	242.12
Etymology	
Aramaic	416
Hebrew	402
Ladino	426
Yiddish	436
European Jewry, see East European Jewry, West European Jewry, Mediterranean Jewry	
Euthanasia	656.3
Exilarch	626
Exile, Babylonian, see Babylonian exile	
Existentialism	180
Exodus (Book of the Bible)	021
Explorers	797
Expulsions	709
Falashas, see Beta Yisrael	
Family and family life	652
Bible	006.21
family histories	798.2
family trees	798.1
in Israel	869
Purity (laws), see Taharat ha-Mishpahah	619.6
Family education	376

Index

Fast days	253
see also individual fast days (e.g., Tishah be-Av)	
Federations (Community)	623
Feminism	619.6
Fertile Crescent, *see* Near East, Ancient	
Festschriften	
general	910
historical	701
Fiction	
anthologies	550.3
criticism	533
history and development	500.3
individual works	563
Finland, Jews in	769.4
First-born, redemption of, *see* Pidyon Ha-Ben	
First Temple (historical period), *see* Temple	
Five Books of Moses, *see* Torah	
Folk dance	695.3
Folk expressions	186
Folk songs	687
Israeli	687.2
Folklore	
anthologies	185.6
Ashkenazic	190
Biblical	187
Chelm stories	190.3
comparative	196
concerning Jews	195
Hasidic	190.5
history	185.7
holidays and festivals	236.85
Israel	194

Folklore (*continued*)
  Oriental   191
  research and criticism   185.5
  Sephardic   189
  study and teaching   185.3
  Talmudic   188
Food
  cooking and culinary arts   699
  customs   615
  Kashrut   221.1
Foundation Fund, *see Keren Ha-Yesod*
France, Jews in   767
Free Loan Societies   638.6
Fund-raising   627
Funeral
  customs   613
  religious rites   222.5
  see also Burial

Galilee   832
Galut (Diaspora Jewry)   724
  Israel, relation with   885
Games
  educational   389
  indoor   696.6
  public   696
Gaonic (Early Talmudic) Period (historical)   729
Gaonim (Babylonian scholars)   126
  codes   126.4
  responsa   126.5
Gaza   838.181
Gedaliah, Fast of   254

Gemara	
history and development	120
see also Talmud	
Gematria	152.2
Genealogy	798.1
General Zionism	811
political party in Israel	843.2
Genesis (Book of the Bible)	020
Genesis Rabbah	141.11
Genetics	602
Genocide	736.02
Geography	
Bible	009.1
Israel	830
Geonim	126
Geriatrics	653
Germany, Jews in	761
Gnosticism	154
non-Jewish	164.1
God (concept)	
anthropomorphism	136.18
Articles of Faith	136.37
attributes	136.1
covenant (*Brit*)	136.31
fear of (*Yirat Shamayim*)	136.3
names	136.12
profanation of God's name	136.79
sanctification of God's name	136.71
Golan Heights	839.5
Government	
in Israel	840

Government (*continued*)	
Jewish community	620
theory	621
Grammar	
Bible	004.8
see also individual languages	
Graphic arts	670
in Israel	884
Graveyards, *see* Cemeteries	
Great Assembly, *see Knesset ha-Gedolah*	
Great Britain, Jews in	766
Greece, Jews in	757.6
Guilds	648.1
Gulf War (1990)	828.55
Habad	213
Habakuk	045
Habimah (Hebrew Theater Company)	883.1
Habonim	812.7
Hadassah	811.6
Haftarot (reading from the prophets in the synagogue)	224.2
Haganah (pre-state defense force)	827.5
Haggadah, *see Aggadah*	
Haggadah, Pesah	244.29
Haggai	047
Haifa	836.14
Haifa University	873.5
Halakhah	100
customs and ceremonies	221
Mishnaic period	112
post-talmudic	125
Hametz (Pesah)	
Bedikat Hametz	244.11

Index

Hamisha Asar Bishvat, *see* Tu Bi-Shevat	
Hammurabi's code	096.1
Handicapped, aid to	638.2
Hanoar Hatzioni	811.8
Hanukkah	247
Hanukkat Habayit (dedication of the home)	223.1
Hashomer Hatzair	812.5
Hasidim, Hasidic movements	213
anti-Hasidic writings	213.9
folklore	190.5
Kabbalah	161
thought	161
Haskalah	734.3
literature	510.8
Hasmoneans	726
Havdalah	237.14
Hazan	636.2
Hazanut (cantorial music)	686.2
Health	
customs	612
in Israel	871
institutions	638
social condition	656
Hebrew Christians, *see* Jewish Christians	
Hebrew Immigrant Aid Society, *see* HIAS	
Hebrew language	400
biblical Hebrew	004
dictionaries	403
idiomatic	404
grammar	408
history and development	400
renaissance of spoken Hebrew	400.5

Hebrew language (*continued*)
  study and teaching
    elementary education   348
    secondary education   359
    self-study texts   409
Hebrew literature
  anthologies   555
  history and development   510
Hebrew schools, afternoon   313.2
  curriculum   336
  see also Schools
Hebrew speaking camps   381.2
Hebrew Union College
  bulletins   369.1
  history   640.4
Hebrew University (Jerusalem)   873.1
Hebron   837.182
Hechalutz Hatzair   812.6
Heder   335.1
Hellenism   660.2
Herut   843.2
Herzl, Theodore
  biographies   799.8
  Zionist theory   802.3
Hevra Kadisha (Burial Society)   638.7
HIAS   638.5
Hibbat Zion   804.1
Hiddushim (Novellae)
  Talmud   101.6
High Holidays   238
  history and development   238.7
  liturgy   238.2
  program materials   238.6

study and teaching	238.3
see also Rosh Hashanah, Yom Kippur, Selihot	
Higher education, *see* Universities and colleges	
Histadrut	863.1
Histadrut Ivrit of America	642
History	
of Israel (state)	820
of the Jewish people	700
Amoraitic period (200–500 CE)	728
contemporary era (20th Century–)	735
emergence of the Jewish people	
(20th–5th Centuries BCE)	710
First Commonwealth	715
medieval	730
normative Judaism (9th–19th Centuries)	730
study and teaching	703
elementary education	349
secondary education	361
Talmud Judaism (5th Century BCE–	
8th Century CE)	720
Tannaitic period (165 BCE–200 CE)	725
Holidays and festivals	
ecumenical	285
Jewish	236
cookery	699.1
folklore	236.85
history and development	236.7
liturgy	236.2
program material	236.6
religious rites	236.1
see also individual holidays	
patriotic (U.S.)	286
post-biblical	246

Holidays and festivals (*continued*)
  study and teaching   236.3
    elementary education   347
    secondary education   357
  universal   287
Holocaust   736
  concentration camps   736.1
  memorials and organizations   736.6
  personal narratives   736.5
  poetry   561.736
  refugees and rescue   736.4
  reparations and restitution   736.8
  resistance   736.2
  Righteous Gentiles   736.41
  revisionism   736.91
  Second Generation   736.93
  special topics   736.9
  war crimes and criminals   736.3
Home
  customs   614
  dedication of, *see* Hanukkat habayit
Homelessness   658.5
Homiletics   202
Hosea   038
Hospitals   638.1
Housing   657
Huleh Valley   833.1
Humanistic Judaism   181.2
Humash (Torah—Five Books of Moses)   015
Humor
  anthologies   550.7
  history and development   500.7
  individual works   567
  see also individual literatures

Hungary, Jews in	762.1
Hygiene	612
Hymns	686.4
Iberian Peninsula	
Jews in	755
Iceland, Jews in	769.5
Idealism	177
Identity, Jewish (non-halakhic)	655
Idolatry	
as opposed to faith and trust in God	136.39
Ignorance	136.69
Illegal immigration	827.9
Immigrants	
in Israel	868
absorption of	868.5
social conditions and problems	868
see also Migrations	
Immigration and emigration	
in Israel	868
history	827
Kibbutz Galuyyot	868.1
laws and policies	604.3
see also Aliyah	
see also Migrations	
Immortality	136.91
Incunabula	943
Independence Day	
Israel	259
U.S.	286
India, Jews in	792.1
Infertility	652.4
Ingathering of the exiles, see Kibbutz Galuyyot	

Inquisition	758.9
Institutions, see Organizations	
Integrated curriculum	331.5
Interdating	652.2
Intermarriage	652.2
Intermediate education, see Elementary education	
International organizations and institutions	644
Intifada	828.54
Investment in Israel	859
Iran	
general	897
Jews in	742
Iraq	
general	896
Jews in	741
Ireland, Jews in	766.7
Irgun Tzeva'i Le'umi	827.5
Irrigation in Israel	857.1
Isaiah	034
Islam	293
impact of the Bible upon	013.1
philosophy	184
Israel, see *Eretz Yisrael*	
for State, see Israel (state)	
Israel, kingdom of	715
Israel (state)	
agriculture	858
anti-Israel propaganda	848.3
Arab relations	890.5
archeology	820.5
arts	880
banks and banking	859

Index

climate	831.3
communications	862
constitution	841
counter-terrorism	890.62
courts	850
culture	875
demography	865
diaspora relations	885
ecology	857.4
economics	855
education	872
higher	873
elections	842.2
emigration	868.9
environment	831
fauna	831.6
finance	846
flora	831.5
foreign relations	848
forests	857.2
geography	830
geology	831
government	840
local	854
health and medical services	871
history (including state and pre-state)	820
housing	856.3
immigration and emigration	868
industry	861
intelligence (military)	849.4
irrigation	857.1
labor and labor organizations	863

Israel (state) (continued)
- land use — 857
- law
  - civil — 851
  - criminal — 851
  - enforcement — 853
  - religious — 852
- legislative process — 844
- libraries — 874
- literature — 511
  - anthologies — 556
- manufacturing — 861
- museums — 874.8
- national observances — 877
- natural history — 831
- natural resources — 831
- parks — 857.3
- political participation — 842
- political parties — 843
- press, publishing, mass media — 878
- public administration — 847
- Rabbinate — 876.4
- refugees — 868
- religion — 876
- science and technology — 864
- security — 849.4
- settlement — 858
- social conditions and problems — 869
- social welfare — 870
- sports and recreation — 879
- study and teaching — 362
- taxation — 846.1

Index

transportation	862
women	866.619
Italy, Jews in	756
Jaffa (Yafo)	836.64
Japan, Jews in	792.3
Jeremiah	035
Jericho	833.481
Jerusalem	837.14
Jerusalem Day, *see* Yom Yerushalayim	
Jerusalem Talmud, *see* Talmud Yerushalmi	
Jesus	292.2
Jewish Agency for Israel	816
Jewish Agricultural Society	647.1
Jewish Brigade	735.3
Jewish Christians	292.6
Jewish Colonial Trust	806.3
Jewish community	
administration	628
communal institutions and organizations	635
councils	624
courts	625
educational institutions	640
external affairs	634
federations and community councils	623
government	620
health and welfare institutions	638
kehillot	623
local governments	623
national and multi-community structures	622
organizations	635
political participation	629

Jewish community (*continued*)
   structure   620
   taxation   627
   theory   621
Jewish Education Service of North America (JESNA)   310.6
Jewish Historical Society of England   706.66
Jewish identity   655
Jewish influence
   of individual Jews   666
   on world civilization   665
Jewish Institute of Religion, *see* Hebrew Union College
Jewish Labor Committee   648.3
Jewish Legion   827.4
Jewish National and University Library   874.1
Jewish National Fund, see *Keren Kayemet le-Yisrael*
Jewish—Non–Jewish Relations   661
Jewish Publication Society of America   941
Jewish Religion (general)   200
Jewish Science   219
Jewish Telegraphic Agency   921.9
Jewish Theological Seminary of America   640.4
Jews for Jesus   292.6
Jews in the world order   660
Jezreel Valley   834
Job   058
Joel   039
Jonah   042
Jordan Valley   833
Joshua   028
Journalism   920
Jubilee year   235.2
Judah, Kingdom of   717.2
Judah Halevi   172

Judaism (religion) 200
   dictionaries and encyclopedias 204
   guides to Jewish living 220
   history 207
   holidays and observances 236
   liturgy 230
   religious movements 210
   study and teaching 203
      elementary 347
      secondary 357
Judea 837
Judean Hills 837.1
Junior congregation 351.2
Justice 136.4
Juvenile delinquency 654
   in Israel 869
Juveniles, *see* Youth

Kabbalah 150
   Abulafian Kabbalah 157
   adaptations, non-Jewish 164
   Geonic Kabbalah 155
   Gnosticism, Jewish 154
   Hasidic Kabbalah 161
   practical Kabbalah 152
   pre-classical Kabbalah 153
   Sephardic Kabbalah 158
   special topics 150.9
   theoretical Kabbalah 151
   Zohar 159
Kaddish (mourner's prayer) 222.5
Kapparot (Yom Kippur) 240.11
Karaism, Karaite Sect 212

Kashrut (dietary laws)	221.1
Kehillah	
see Jewish Community	
Keren Ami	350.1
Keren Ha-Yesod (Foundation Fund)	818
Keren Kayemet le-Yisrael (Jewish National Fund)	817
Ketubbah (marriage document)	222.4
Ketuvim (Writings, Hagiographa)	050
Kevutzah (collective settlement)	858.6
Kibbutz (collective settlement)	858.6
Kibbutz Galuyyot (Ingathering of the Exiles)	868.1
Kiddush Levanah (blessing of the moon)	265
Kindergarten	342
curriculum	332
in Israel	872
Kings (Books of the Bible)	032, 033
Kinneret (Lake), *see* Sea of Galilee	
Kipah (skull cap)	225.1
Kiryat *Shemonah*	833.152
Kitzur Shulhan Arukh	129.5
Knesset (Parliament, Israel)	844
Knesset ha-Gedolah	624
Kol Nidre	238.2
sacred music	686
Kol Yisrael (Radio Israel)	878.5
Koran	293.1
Kriat ha-Torah (Reading from the Torah)	224.1
Kuppat Holim (Health insurance in Israel)	871.5
Labor	648
in Bible	011
in Israel	863
in Talmud	101.9

Labor movements
  in the diaspora   648.3
  in Israel   863
Labor unions   648.2
  in Israel   863
Labor Zionism   812
  see also Po'alei Zion
Ladino
  language   425
  literature   501
  songs   687.3
Lag Ba-omer   250
Lamentations (Book of the Bible)   062
Land reclamation in Israel   857
Landsmannschaften   639.3
Language of the Jews
  Aramaic   415
  Hebrew   400
  Ladino   425
  other   445
  Yiddish   435
Latin America
  Jews in   785
  literature   558
Latvia, Jews in   763.4
Law
  as an occupation   647.4
  biblical   011.1
  codification   125.4
    Aharonim   130
    Geonim   126
    Mishneh Torah   128
    Rishonim   127.4

Law (*continued*)
    Shulhan Arukh   129
    comparative   134
    contemporary   131
    in Israel   844
    Jewish, general   100
    oral   100
    see also *Halakhah*; Talmud
    reading of (*Kriat ha-Torah*)   224.1
League of Nations and Palestine   827.4
Learning
    concept   136.65
Learning disabled, education   388
Learning theory   392
Leaven, *see Hametz*
Leaven, search for, *see Bedikat Hametz*
Lebanon
    general   894
    Jews in   754
Legends, *see* Folklore
Legislation
    in Israel   844
    in Jewish community   624
Levites   006.33
Leviticus (Book of the Bible)   022
    Vayikrah Rabbah   141.13
Liberal movements in Judaism   217
    in Israel   876.3
    thought   176
    see also Reform Movement in Judaism
Libraries   640.3
    in Israel   874

Index

Library Automation	970.4
Library Science	970
for Judaica	980
Likud (political party in Israel)	843.2
Linguistics	400
biblical	004
Talmud	102.4
Literature, general	
encyclopedias/dictionaries	905
related to Jews and Judaism	590
Literature, Jewish	500
study and teaching	540
secondary education	360
Lithuania, Jews in	763.7
Liturgical music, see Hazanut	
Liturgy	230
Ashkenazic	232
concept of prayer (*Tefilah*)	136.55
Conservative, nontraditional	234.3
Conservative, traditional	232
history and development	230.7
Reconstructionist	234.2
Reform	234.1
Sephardic	231
study and teaching	230.3
elementary education	347
secondary education	357
see also individual holidays and festivals	
Local government	
in Israel	854
Jewish community	623
Lod (Lydda)	835.351

Logic
  Jewish thought   135.8
  Talmudic   102.7
Lulav   242.12
Luxembourg, Jews in   768.3

Maccabean revolt   726.1
Maccabees
  Books of Apocrypha   078, 079, 086, 087
  historical period   722.3
Maccabiah (Jewish Olympics)   696.6
Magen David (Star of David)   225.3
Magen David Adom ("Red Cross" in Israel)   871.7
Maggid   601.6
Magic   164.5
Mahzor (festival prayerbook), *see* liturgy of
  individual festivals
Maimonides, *see* Moses Ben Maimon
Maki (Israel Communist Party)   843.4
Malachi   049
Mandatory Palestine   827.5
Manuscripts   942
Mapai (political party in Israel)   843.1
Mapam (political party in Israel)   843.1
Maps   967
  Israel   830.5
Marranos   758
Marriage   652
  religious rites   222.4
Martyrs   709
Masada   824.3
Mathematics
  as a profession   647.6
  Bible   012.4

Matzah (unleavened bread), *see* Pesah
Medical Ethics	490.5
Medicine	490
as an occupation	647.5
Bible	012.1
customs	612
in Israel	871
institutions	638
Medieval history of the Jews	730

Mediterranean Jewry, *see* Sephardic and Mediterranean Jewry

Mekhilta	114.1
Memorials (World War II)	736.6
Menorah	225.2
Hanukkah	247.1
Mental health	656.1
Mentally handicapped, education	387
Merchant	
as an occupation	647.3
Meshek Shittufi (collective farm)	858.7
Messianism	
concept	136.9
movements (historical)	207.8
Metal arts	678
Metullah	833.151
Mexico, Jews in	787.1
Mezuzah	223.1
Middle East	890
peace process	828.6, 890.51
Middle Eastern Jewry (excluding Mediterranean countries)	
customs (social)	610
ethnography	603

Middle Eastern Jewry (*continued*)
   history   740
   languages   445
   liturgy   233
   social history   601
Midrash Rabbah   141.1
Midrashic literature, *see* Aggadah
   biblical   141
   ethical   142
   festival   143
   Halakhic   114
   historical   144
   post-classical   145
Migrations   604
Mikveh (ritual bath)
   construction   673.6
   halakhah   221.5
Military
   Bible   006.4
   Israel   849
Minyan (quorum for conducting public worship)   224.3
Miracles (*Nissim*)   136.22
   in the Bible   007
Mishkan (Tabernacle)   006.6
Mishnah   110
Mishneh Torah   128
Missions, Christian   661.9
   in Israel   876.6
Mitnagdim (opponents of the Hasidim)   733
   writings   213.9
Mitzvot (commandments)
   as a concept   136.7
   Taryag Mitzvot (613 commandments)   125.1

Index

Mixed marriage, see Intermarriage	
Mizrachi (National Religious Political Party in Israel)	843.3
Mizrachi (Religious Zionist Organization)	813.3
Mo'ed (Order of the Babylonian Talmud)	105
Mo'ed (Order of the Jerusalem Talmud)	115.4
Mo'ed (Order of the Mishnah)	110.4
Mohammedanism, see Islam	
Mohel, see Brit Milah	
Moldovia, Jews in	764.7
Monarchy	006.12
Moneylending	647.3
Monotheism	
comparative religion	290.9
Judaism	206
Moon, blessing of the, see Kiddush Levanah; Birkat ha-Hodesh	
Mormonism	292.69
Morocco, Jews in	753
Mortara Case	662.52
Moses	021.8
Assumption of Moses	084.2
Moses Ben Maimon (Maimonides)	
biography	173
commentary on the Mishnah	110.2
medical works	480
Mishneh Torah	128
philosophy	173
Moses, Five Books of, see Torah	
Moshava (collective farm)	858.5
Moshav Ovdim (collective farm)	858.7
Motion pictures	692

Mourning	
customs	613
religious rites	222.5
Movies, *see* Motion pictures	
Musar movement	733
Museums	
in Israel	874.8
museumology	995
Music	685
dramatic	688
folk	687
instrumental	689
in Israel	882
sacred	686
study and teaching	339.3
vocal	687
Musicals	688.3
Muslim-Jewish relations	661.5
Mysticism, *see* Kabbalah	
Mysticism, non-Kabbalistic	182
Nabateans	824.5
Naggid	626
Nahal	849.8
Nahariyya	832.351
Nahum (Book of the Bible)	044
Names and naming	222.11
Names of God, *see* God, names	
Nashim (Order of the Babylonian Talmud)	106
Nashim (Order of the Jerusalem Talmud)	115.5
Nashim (Order of the Mishnah)	110.5
Nasi	626
National Conference of Christians and Jews	661.3

National Council of Jewish Women	639
National Federation of Hebrew Teachers and Principals	310.6
National Jewish Welfare Board	642
National Religious Party, see Mizrachi	
National Socialism, see Nazism	
Natural history	
Bible	009
Israel (state)	831
Talmud	101.9
Nazareth	832.251
Nazi Holocaust, see Holocaust	
Nazism	736.01
neo-Nazism	662.96
Near East	
ancient	090
modern	890
Needlework	680.3
Negev	838
Nehemiah (Book of the Bible)	067
Neo-Nazism	662.96
Ner Tamid (Eternal Light)	224
Netanyah	836.454
Netherlands, Jews in	768.1
Neturei Karta (right wing religious group)	876.2
Nevi'im (Prophets)	025
New Christians, see Marranos	
New Moon, see Rosh Hodesh	
New Moon, Blessing of the, see Rosh Hodesh	
New Testament, see Christian Scriptures	
New Year, see Rosh Ha-Shanah	
New Year for Trees, see Tu Bi-Shevat	
New Zealand, Jews in	794.2

New Zionist Organization, *see* Revisionism
Newspapers — 921
Nezikin (Order of the Babylonian Talmud) — 107
Nezikin (Order of the Jerusalem Talmud) — 115.6
Nezikin (Order of the Mishnah) — 110.6
NILI — 827.4
Ninth of Av, *see* Tishah Be-Av
Noahide Laws — 136.88
Normative Judaism (historical period) — 730
North Africa, Jews in — 752
Norway, Jews in — 769.2
Novellae, *see* Hiddushim
Novels, *see* Fiction
Numbers (Book of the bible) — 023
Numismatics — 676
Nursery Schools
   administration — 315.5
   curriculum — 332.1
   in Israel — 872
   methodology — 341

Obadiah — 041
Occupations — 647
   in the Bible — 007
Olam Ha-ba (world to come) — 136.93
Old age homes — 638.3
Old Testament, *see* Bible
Omer, counting of, *see* Sefirat ha-Omer
Oneg Shabbat — 237.6
Online searching
   general — 976.1
   Jewish — 985.1

Index

Opera	688.1
Operation Ezra and Nehemiah	868
Operation Magic Carpet	868
Oral history	989.1
Oratorios	868.6
Ordination, see Semikhah	
Organizations	
cultural	642
educational	640
health	638
international	644
religious	
synagogue	636
"representative" and political purpose	637
service	639
social	643
welfare	638
youth	641
Oriental Jewry, see also Sephardic and Mediterranean Jewry	
cookery	699.2
folklore	191
literature	502
anthologies	552
liturgy	231
Oriental religions	294
Origami	679.4
ORT (Organization for Rehabilitation and Training)	644
Orthodox Movement in Judaism	214
in Israel	876.2
thought	179
Oslo Peace Accords	828.6

Paganism	291
Pageants	691.2
Pakistan, Jews in	792.1
Pales of Settlement (Russia)	764
Palestine, see *Eretz Yisrael*, Israel (state); Mandatory Palestine	
Palestine Liberation Organization	890.61
see also Palestinian Authority	
Palestinian Arabs	890.6
Palestinian Authority	890.6
Palmach	827.9
Parenting	652.7
Pareveh (neither meat nor milk)	221.1
Parliament, Israeli, see *Knesset*	
Parties, political	
Israel	843
see also Political behavior of the Jews	
Partisans	736.2
Partition of Palestine	827.9
Paschal Lamb, see Pesah	
Passover, see Pesah	
Penitence, Ten Days of, see *Aseret Yemei Teshuvah*	
Periodicals	921
directories	921.6
indexes	921.3
literary (including selections)	580
Persia, Jews in	742
Pesah	244
cookery	699.11
Haggadah	244.29
Pesiktot	143
Petah Tikvah	836.657
Pharisees	725.1

Index

Pharmacy (as an occupation)	647.5
Philanthropy	
concept, see *Tzedakah*	
operation, see Fund-raising	
Philippines, Jews in	794.3
Philistines	822
as related to Bible	095
Philo	165.8
Philosophy	
comparative	184
medieval	170
modern	175
Phoenicians	095.72
Photography	683
Phylacteries, see *Tefillin*	
Physically handicapped, education	386
Pictures	
teaching aids, see Audiovisual education	
Pidyon ha-Ben (redemption of the First Born)	222.2
Pilgrimage festivals, see *Shalosh Regalim*	
Pilpul (Talmudic discussion)	102.7
Pioneer Women	812.8
Pirkei Avot	107.12
Piyyutim	230.8
Plagues, Ten	244.7
Plastic arts	675
in Israel	884
Plays (drama)	691.1
Poale Mizrachi	813.4
Po'alei Zion	812.4
Poetry	
anthologies	550.1
Hebrew	510

Poetry (*continued*)
   history and development   500.1
   Ladino   501
   Yiddish   503
   see also specific literatures
Poland, Jews in   763.6
Political behavior of the Jews   668
Polygamy   652.9
   in the Bible   012
   in the Talmud   101.9
   Post-Talmudic Halakhah   125.9
Polyglot Bibles   001.5
Poor, *see* Poverty
Population studies   606
Poskim, see Law, codification
Postage stamps
   collections   682.9
   see also Postal service
Postal service in Israel   862.6
Poverty
   Jewish attitude toward   667
   social conditions and problems   658.5
Prayer (liturgy)   230
   as a concept (*tefilah*)   136.55
Prayer books, *see Siddurim*
Prayer shawl, *see Tallit*
President of Israel (office)   845.1
Press
   in Israel   878
   Jewish journalism   920
Press services   921.9
Priests and Priesthood   006.32

Printing	941
Pronunciation	
Hebrew language	406.1
Yiddish language	441
Prophets (Books in the Bible)	025
Proselytes, *see* Conversion to Judaism	
Proselytizing of Jews	661.9
Provence, Jews in	767.9
Proverbs (Books of the Bible)	057
Proverbs (folk expressions)	186
Psalms (Book of the Bible)	056
Publishing	941
Purim	249
Pseudepigrapha	080
Psychiatry	399
Psychoanalysis	399
Psychology	390
child	397
group	396
self-help	398
Puppetry	679.3
Quiz Books	203.05
Quorum for conducting public worship	
see Minyan	
Quotations	550.8
Rabbinate (Synagogue)	636.2
Israel	876.4
Rabbinical Assembly of America	636.27
Rabbinical courts	625
in Israel	852

Rabbinical Seminaries	640.1
in Israel	873.9
Racial group, *see* Ethnography	
Radio	693
in Israel	878.5
Rambam, *see* Moses ben Maimon	
Ramleh	835.352
Ram's horn, *see* Shofar	
Rare books	943–949
Reader's Theater	351.5
Reading of the law, *see* Kriat Ha-Torah	
Reclamation, land *see* Land reclamation	
Reconstructionist Movement in Judaism	216
liturgy	234.2
thought	181.1
Records	964
"Red Cross" in Israel, *see* Magen David Adom	
Redemption of the first born, *see* Pidyon ha-Ben	
Reform Judaism, *see* Reform Movement in Judaism	
Reform Movement in Judaism	217
in Israel	876.3
liturgy	234.1
thought	176
Refugees	
Arab, *see* Arab refugees	
Holocaust	736.4
in Israel	868
studies	604.5
Rehovot	836.755
Religion	
comparative	290
in Israel	876

Courts	852
law	852
non-Jewish	876.6
Jewish, *see* Judaism	
Religious freedom	
in Israel	850.5
in Jewish community	630
Religious Naturalism	181
Religious Zionism	813
Reparations and restitution (Holocaust)	736.8
Repentence (*Teshuvah*)	136.56
"Representative" and political purpose organizations	637
Bible	006
Resistance, Jewish (World War II)	736.2
Responsa	125.5
Aharonim	130.5
Contemporary	131.5
Conservative	131.53
Orthodox	131.51
Reconstructionist	131.55
Reform	131.54
Traditional	131.52
Geonim	126.5
Rishonim	127.5
Resurrection	136.94
Revelation	136.13
Revisionism (Holocaust)	736.91
Revisionists (Zionist party)	814.3
Reward and Punishment	136.5
Rhodes (Armistice) Agreements	828.13
Righteous Gentiles	736.41
Rishon Le-Zion	836.752

Rishonim (Talmudic commentators)	127
Codes	127.4
Responsa	127.5
Ritual	
bath, *see* Mikveh	
murder libel, *see* Anti-Semitism	
slaughter, *see* Shehitah	
Rosh Hashanah	239
customs and ceremonies	239.1
history and development	239.7
liturgy	238.2
program material	239.6
see also High Holidays	
study and teaching	239.3
Rosh Hodesh (beginning of a new month)	265
Rosh Pinnah	833.154
Rumania, Jews in	763.8
Russia, Jews in	764
immigration to Israel	868
Saadia Gaon	
philosophy	171
Sabbath, *see* Shabbat	
Sabbatical year	235.2
Saboraim	126
Sacrifices	
Bible	006.31
comparative religion	290.9
Talmud	101.9
Sadducees	722.2
Safed	832.151
Salting of meat, *see* Kashrut	
Samaria	835

Samaritans	211
in Israel	876.6
Sanhedrin	624.1
Grand (France)	767.4
Satire, *see* Humor	
Sayings of the Fathers, *see* Avot, Masekhot	
School	
administration	315
community relations	321
discipline	327
equipment	320
facility planning	318
libraries	
general	971.1
Jewish	987
subjects	
curriculum	330
transportation	319
Schools	
community	313.21
day	313.1
for teachers	640.2
Hebrew	
afternoon	313.2
Israel	872
secular	313.4
synagogue	313.22
Sunday	313.3
Yiddish	313.41
Science	
as an occupation	647.6
Talmudic	103.6

Sciences, Jewish	480
translations	480.6
Scientists	
biography, collective	480.798
biography, individual	480.799
Scotland, Jews in	766.6
Scribes (writing of the Torah)	017.9
Sculpture	675
Sea of Galilee	833.2
Seals	675.2
Second Generation (Holocaust)	736.93
Second Temple (historical period), *see* Temple	
Secondary education	355
curriculum	334
in Israel	872
Secular Jewish thought	183
Sedarot	015
stories on	015.91
Seder (Pesah)	244.12
Sefer Yetzirah	151.5
Sefirat ha-Omer (Counting of the Omer)	244.9
Self-government, *see* Jewish Community	
Selihot	238.29
Semikhah, *see* Rabbinical Seminaries	
Seminaries	
Rabbinical	640.1
teachers	640.2
Semitic languages	455
Sephardic and Mediterranean Jewry	750
cookery	669.2
customs (social)	610
dispersion	759
ethnography	603

Index

history	750
literature	501
anthologies	551
liturgy	231
social history	601
Septuagint	003.8
Serbia, Jews in	757.71
Serials	921
Sermons	202
Service organizations (e.g., *B'nai B'rith*)	639
Settlement patterns	657
Settlements, agricultural	
in Israel	858
in the diaspora, *see* individual communities	
Sex	
behavior	651
customs	611
Shabbat	237
customs and ceremonies	237.1
history and development	237.7
literature	237.5
liturgy	237.2
program material	237.6
study and teaching	237.3
Shabbat *ha-Gadol*	237.96
Shabbateans	207.8
Shabbatot, special	237.9
Shalom Ha-Galil Campaign (Lebanon War, 1982)	828.53
Shalosh Regalim (Pilgrimage Festivals)	241
see also individual holidays	
Shavuot	245
Shehitah (ritual slaughter)	221.1
Shemini Atzeret	243

Shivah Asar B'Tammuz	257
Shofar (Ram's horn)	238.11
artistic	675.3
Shulhan Arukh	129
Shushan Purim	249.9
Siddurim (Prayer Books)	231.1
Sifra	114.2
Sifrei	114.3
Simhat Torah	243
Sin	136.78
Sinai Campaign (1956)	828.23
Sinai Peninsula	838.5
Sins, casting of, *see Tashlich*	
Sisterhood (synagogue)	636.3
Six Day War (1967)	828.33
Six hundred and thirteen commandments, *see Taryag Mitzvot*	
Social	
behavior	600
conditions	650
Bible	006.2
Israel	869
Jewish response to	667
history	601
institutions	600
problems	650
services	638.5
as an occupation	647.7
Songs	
literature, *see* Poetry	
music	687
South America, Jews in	785
Spain, Jews in	755

Index

Sports	696
in Israel	879
Stamps	
metallic, see Seals	
postage, see Postage Stamps	
Statistics	
Israel	865
social	605
vital (population statistics)	606
Stone carving	675.5
Story-telling	351.6
Student Zionist Organization	810.8
Study and learning (concept)	136.65
Suicide	656.6
Sukkah	242.11
Sukkot	242
customs and ceremonies	242.1
history and development	242.7
liturgy	242.2
program material	242.6
study and teaching	242.3
Summer camps	381
Sweden, Jews in	769.1
Switzerland, Jews in	762.2
Synagogue	
architecture	672
as a community institution	636
history	636.7
observances, practices, rites	224
Synagogue (Assembly), the Great, see Knesset ha-Gedolah	
Syria, Jews in	754
general	894

Ta'anit Ester	256
Tabernacle, *see* Mishkan	
Tabernacles (holiday), *see* Sukkot	
Tables, Historical	705
Tabor (Mt.)	834.1
Taharat Ha-Mishpahah (Laws of Family Purity)	221.5
Tallit (prayer-shawl)	221.3
Talmud	
anthologies	101.2
biography	103.7
commentaries	101
concordances	102.6
criticism	103
dictionaries	102.5
history and development	103.7
language	102.4
method and system	102.7
research	103
study aids	102
Yerushalmi (Jerusalem)	115
Talmud, burning of	709
Talmudic period (history)	720
in *Eretz Yisrael*	823
Tammuz, 17th of, *see Shivah Asar B'Tammuz*	
Tanakh, *see* Bible	
Tannaim	111.7
Tannaitic period (historical 165 BCE–200 CE)	725
Taryag Mitzvot (613 Commandments)	125.1
Tashlikh (casting of the sins)	239.11
Taxation	
Israel	846.1
Jewish community	627

Index

Teachers
  training   326
Teachers' seminaries   640.2
  in Israel   873.8
Teaching   325
Technion (Haifa)   873.2
Technology
  as an occupation   647.6
  Bible   012.3
Tefillin (Phylacteries)   221.2
Tel Aviv-Jaffa (Yafo)   836.64
Tel Aviv University   873.4
Television   693
  in Israel   878.5
Temple
  First (historical period)   717
  Second (historical period)   721
Temple (institution)   006.7
Ten Commandments, *see Aseret ha-Dibbrot*
Ten Lost Tribes
  folklore   187.5
Terrorism and territories, Arab   890.61
Testaments of the Twelve Patriarchs   082.1
Testing (education)   329
Textbooks
  elementary education   340.3
  secondary education   355.3
Theater
  in Israel   883
  Jewish   691
Theology, general concepts   136
  non-Jewish   290.3
  see also God, Judaism

Thirteen Articles of Faith (Maimonides)	173.2
Thought, Jewish	
general	135
Hellenistic	165
medieval	170
modern	175
Tiberias	833.251
Tishah be-Av	258
Tishri (Hebrew month)	277
Tohorot (Order of the Mishnah)	110.8
Torah (Five Books of Moses, Pentateuch)	015
see also Bible	
commentaries	016
concordances	017.5
criticism	018
dictionaries	017.4
polyglot	015.5
reading from the Torah	224.1
research	018
special topics	019.9
translation from Hebrew	015.2
writing of	017.9
Torah (concept)	136.6
Torah academies, *see* Yeshivot	
Tosefta	121
Trade unions, *see* Labor unions	
Tradition, Jewish, *see* Judaism	
Transjordan	839
Translations, scientific (classical)	480.6
Translations of the Bible, *see* Bible	
Travel and travelers	797
Travel guides	796
Israel	830.7

Index

Tribal confederacy (historical period and political system)	716
Tribes, lost ten (folklore), *see* Ten Lost Tribes	
Tribes and the tribal system	006.11
Tribunals	625
Triennial cycle, *see* Law, reading of	
Tu be-Av	251
Tu Bi-Shevat	248
Turkey, Jews in	757.5
general	898
Twelve Tribes, *see* Tribes and the tribal system	
Tzedakah	
concept	136.4
institutions	638
in Israel	870
Tzeva Haganah Le-Israel (Israeli defense forces)	849
Tzimtzum	150.9
Tzitzit (Tallit)	221.3
Tzom Gedaliah	254
Ukraine, Jews in	764.6
Ulpan (intensive Hebrew course)	872.6
Union catalogs	959
Union of American Hebrew Congregations	636.87
Union of Orthodox Jewish Congregation of America	636.87
Union of Orthodox Rabbis of U.S. and Canada	636.27
Union of Sephardi Congregations	636.87
Unions, Labor	648.2
in Israel	863
United Hias Service, *see* HIAS	
United Israel Appeal, *see* United Jewish Appeal	
United Jewish Appeal	627
United Nations and Israel	848.95
United Services for New Americans, *see* HIAS	

United States, Jews in
  communal institutions and organizations   635.9
  cultural institutions and organizations   642.7
  customs (social)   610
  economic conditions   646.7
  education   310
  educational institutions and organizations   640
  ethnography   603
  health and welfare institutions   638
  history   770
    1621–1918   771
    1918–   772
  literature   520
  service organizations   639.7
  social conditions and problems   650.7
  social organizations   643.7
  States of the Union   773–780.6
United Synagogue of America   636.87
United Zionists-Revisionists, *see* Revisionists
Universities and colleges
  administration   367
  curriculum   366
  in Israel   873
  publications   369

Vaad Ha-Lashon Ha-Ivrit (Academy of the Hebrew Language)   400.6
Video cassettes   961
Visiting the sick, *see* Bikkur Holim
Vocal music, *see* Songs
Vocalization of Hebrew (*Nikkud*)   401.5
Vowels, *see* Vocalization

Index

War criminals (Nazis)	736.3
Warfare	
Bible	006.4
Jewish response	667
War of Attrition	828.3
War of Independence (1948–1949)	828.13
Wedding, see Marriage	
Weeks, Feast of, see Shavuot	
Weights and measures	
Bible	011
Talmud	101.9
Weizmann Institute of Science	873.3
Welfare institutions	638
Welfare in Israel	870
West Bank, see Judea, Samaria	
West European Jewry	
customs (social)	610
ethnography	603
history	765
literature	504, 522
social history	601
Western Wall	837.145
White Paper of 1939	827.7
"Who is a Jew"	655
Widowhood	652.6
Wisdom literature	055
Witchcraft	164.4
WIZO	811.7
Women	
Bible	006.22
biography	008
customs and ceremonies	619.2
feminism	619.6

Women (continued)
  in Israel   866.619
  position and treatment   619
  responsa   125.5
  Talmud   101.9
Woodcarving   675.4
Workmen's Circle   648.37
World Jewish Congress   637
World War I   735.1
  Israel   827.4
World War II   735.3
  Israel   827.8
World Zionist Congress   806.1
World Zionist Organization   806
Writings (Books of the Bible), see Ketuvim
Written law, see Bible

Yahrzeit   222.5
Yamim Noraim (High Holidays)   238
Yarmulka   225.1
Yearbooks
  general   909
  Jewish   915–925
Yemen
  General   899.5
  Jews in   744
Yemenite Jewry
  Israel, community in   869
  literature   502
  liturgy   233; 237.23
  Yemen, community in   744
Yeshivot (Talmud academies)
  curriculum   335.1

Index

day schools	313.1
history	640
Israel	308, 872
U.S.	640.1
Yiddish	
language	435
literature	503
schools, afternoon	313.41
curriculum	338
schools, day	313.41
curriculum	335.6
songs	687.4
YIVO	640.7
Yizkor	232
Yom Ha-Atzma'ut (Israel Independence Day)	259
Yom Ha-Sho'ah U'Gevurah (Holocaust Remembrance and Heroism Day)	260
Yom Ha-Zikkaron (Remembrance Day for Israeli Soldiers)	261
Yom Kippur	240
customs and ceremonies	240.1
history and development	240.7
liturgy	238.2
study and teaching	240.3
Yom Kippur War (1973)	828.43
Yom Yerushalayim (Jerusalem Day)	262
Young Israel	636.8
Young Judaea	811.9
Youth	
movements	
history	641
organization and function	382
Zionist (Non-Party)	810

Youth (*continued*)
   services   638.4
   sociology   650
   see also names of individual movements
Youth Aliyah   868
Yugoslavia, Jews in   757.7

Zealots   722
Zechariah   048
Zemirot   237.6
Zera'im (Order of Babylonian Talmud)   104
Zera'im (Order of the Jerusalem Talmud)   115.3
Zera'im (Order of the Mishnah)   110.3
Zikhron Ya'akov   836.351
Zion Mule Corps   827.4
Zionism, *see also* specific parties and organizations   800
   directories   806.2
   federations   806.9
   history   804
   parties and popular organizations   810
   philosophy   802
   study and teaching   803
Zionist banks   806.3
Zionist Commission   827.5
Zionist Congress   806.1
Zionist Organization of America   806.27
Zionist Renaissance
   literature   510.9
Zionist summer camps   381.3
Zohar   159
Zugot (Paris)   111.7

About the Authors

Professor Daniel J. Elazar received his M.A. and Ph.D. in Political Science from the University of Chicago and is a member of Phi Beta Kappa, the nation's highest academic honorary society.

Professor Elazar is the founder and President of the Jerusalem Center for Public Affairs, the Senator N.M. Paterson Professor at Bar Ilan University, and Director of the Center for Study of Federalism at Temple University. He is the founder and editor of the *Jerusalem Letter/Viewpoints* series, and the *Jewish Political Studies Review*. He is the author or editor of more than 60 books and many other publications, such as *Community and Polity, Understanding the Jewish Agency; Two Peoples—One Land: Federal Solutions for Israel, the Palestinians and Jordan; Covenant and Polity in Biblical Israel;* and *Israel: Building a New Society*.

He currently lives in Jerusalem with his wife Harriet. They have three children.

David Elazar received his B.A. in Chemistry from Wayne State University (Detroit) in 1964, and in 1965, on a Special Libraries Association Scholarship, completed his M.A. in Library Science at the University of Michigan.

In 1970, Elazar moved to Israel, where, until 1981, he held the position of Information Officer at Israel Aircraft Industries' Technical Information Center. In 1981, he was appointed manager of the Center.

As an Information Specialist, he is a member of the Special Libraries Association, the American Society for Information Science, the Israel Society of Special Libraries and Information Centers, and the Association of Jewish Librarians. In the area of aerospace, his memberships include the American Institute of Aeronautics and Astronautics, the Association of Unmanned Vehicles, the International Federation of Airworthiness, and the Royal Aeronautical Society.